THE SEVENTEENTH CENTURY

DIRECTIONS OLD AND NEW

Essays edited by Elizabeth Moles
and Noël Peacock

UNIVERSITY OF GLASGOW FRENCH & GERMAN PUBLICATIONS

1992

University of Glasgow French and German Publications

Series Editors: Mark G. Ward (German)
Geoff Woollen (French)

Consultant Editors : Colin Smethurst
Kenneth Varty

Modern Languages Building, University of Glasgow,
Glasgow G12 8QL, Scotland.

First published 1992.

Cover: Engraving after Dughet, *A Tempest*. © Copyright, and reproduced by kind permission of, the British Museum, London (negative 038989).

Printed by Castle Cary Press, Somerset BA7 7AN.

ISBN 0 85261 344 X

Contents

Acknowledgments

The editors of this volume of essays wish to record their grateful thanks to the following:

The contributors, for their commitment and their cooperation, often during busy teaching periods.

The Courtauld Institute of Art, the Fitzwilliam Museum, Cambridge, and the British Museum, for their kind permission to reproduce Plates 1-4 of Dr. Pace's article and the cover illustration.

Dr Stephen Rawles, Dr Geoff Woollen and Mrs Sandra Peacock, for their generous help with the preparaion of this volume.

Peter and Sue James, and their excellent team of printers at Castle Cary Press.

Directions old and new

This is the first of what is hoped will be a series of biennial conferences on seventeenth-century French studies. The topic, 'Orientations anciennes et nouvelles', was deliberately chosen for a time when the value of literary studies and art history is under sustained and systematic attack. The conference brought together in the University of Glasgow seventeenth-century specialists from as far afield as Aberdeen, East Anglia and Oxford, whose critical approaches ranged from the urbane, traditional *orientation ancienne* of seventeenth-century studies to the more arcane and problematical *orientation nouvelle*.

'La Fontaine's Fable II, 4 and French Classicism' (Christopher Smith) provided an appropriate opening: the poet, who pillaged and caricatured the moral saws of his ancient precursors, is indeed a writer for all seasons: the flip ironies and deprecatory asides of this 'papillon de Parnasse' could well console any 'littérateur' who feels marginalised in straitened times. After setting the reliance of French Classicism on ancient sources in its complex and disturbing historical background, Smith shows how La Fontaine adapts the traditional moralising purpose of the fable in an age demanding 'de la nouveauté et de la gaieté'. Novelty is achieved by witty foregrounding of the animals' sexual identities and separate roles in battle. Moreover, the pessimistic political inferences which the reader is invited to draw both from the moral and from the poet's loaded choice of vocabulary and register are brought into more acute focus. Thus a new orientation is imparted both to ancient form, and to well-worn philosophical content.

The category of seventeenth-century landscape painting, disparaged by contemporary critics, is rehabilitated by Claire Pace ('"Paysage héroïque": seventeenth-century and more recent perceptions of Poussin's landscapes'). The first part of her paper traces the complex meanderings of landscape classification in Félibien, Testelin and de Piles, highlighting the inherently subversive quality of landscape painting, its freedom from the rules governing biblical or mythical subject matter. The second part investigates specific examples, notably *Landscape with Man Killed by a Snake* and *Landscape with a Storm*. Traditional criticism foregrounded the allegorical significance of storms as tempests of fortune, as images of passion and blindness: frail man is buffeted by a thunderbolt and forked lightning. More recent interpretations, however, have stressed Poussin's links with the *libertins*, citing his adherence to the neo-stoic belief that man must stand firm against the storms of fortune. Similarly, the snake was a pictograph of mortality for Poussin's circle, familiar with Egyptian hieroglyphs, whereas modern critics view the snake landscapes as a wider allegory of natural processes expressed in hieroglyphic form.

Descartes and Pascal give an *orientation nouvelle* to orthodox scholastic philosophy and traditional Christian apologetic respectively. In a post-structuralist analysis of traditional metaphors ('Descartes and Pascal: metaphorical sabotage by stealth') Elizabeth Moles unlocks the 'différence' between Descartes and Pascal: Pascal structures both certain key arguments and his chain and building metaphors in opposition to those of Descartes, but too often tries to rout his precursor's logic by mere metaphor. The 'règle des partis' is substituted for the austere 'règles de la méthode'.

In Cornelian criticism, Barthes and Fumaroli have demonstrated a shift away from the traditional emphasis on the platitudes of 'gloire' and 'devoir' to illusionistic effects (particularly in *L'Illusion comique*) and the hollowness of the persuasive rhetoric employed by kings and emperors. William Dickson ('Corneille: the spoken and the unspoken') examines the characters' economies with the truth and alerts us to the folly of attaching importance to a literal interpretation (*orientation ancienne*) of their persuasive strategies and to the need to respond to the dramatic implications of their actions (*orientation nouvelle*). The elevation of their language should not blind us to the gaps in a discourse which is belied by their deeds.

Fourberie in Molière has traditionally been synonymous with rascality. But as Robert McBride argues ('"Toujours par quelque endroit fourbes se laissent prendre": the case of Alceste and his *fourbe*'), the *fourbe*, if absent from the stage in *Le Misanthrope*, is omnipotent and exhibits traits of the *imaginaire* as he unites, in an unlikely and an unholy triumvirate, judge, *honnête homme* and hypocrite. In this analysis of the comedy, both the self-confessed idealist and the *fourbe* equally sport their masks. The triumph of the *fourbe*, a secular Tartuffe, reflects the shift in Molière's 'comic vision' from the *Écoles* which end on a note of self-deflation.

Nicholas Cronk's rehabilitation of *Les Amants magnifiques* ('The Celebration of Carnival in Molière-Lully's *Les Amants magnifiques*') takes as its *point de départ* the innovative 1988 production by the Limoges-based Compagnie Fiévet-Paliès which was taken to Paris to the Théâtre de l'Athénée in 1989. The application of Bakhtin's method to this neglected *comédie-ballet* suggests a fresh perspective on the play's unity and shows how language is relativised by both dance and music (language is 'reduced to the status of spectacle, a medium to be used with relish, but certainly not one which can accord us privileged access to truth'). Carnivalistic laughter is directed towards a shift of world orders: it offers paradoxically a challenge to the authority of the royal remit to 'donner à sa cour un divertissement qui fût composé de tous ceux que le théâtre peut fournir [...]'.

Christine McGarry, one of the research students attending the conference, has another look at 'The Role of the Past in Racine's *Andromaque*'. Focussing on the relationship of the characters' ancestral past with the structure of the plot, she shows the bad faith of Pyrrhus, Hermione and Oreste in their use of the past as a shallow justification for their present actions, and contrasts this with Andromaque's genuine attachment to the past. Yet even the eponymous heroine makes a futile attempt to exploit the pathetic potential of the past by beseeching Hermione to intercede for her with Pyrrhus. Part of the discovery the spectators of the play make is how little power the characters have over their past. McGarry invites us to discern a subtle irony in Racine's use of the past: all his characters use it as a strategic ploy but in reality the very grip the past exercises over them defeats their best rhetorical endeavour in the pursuit of their selfish aims. Her analyses of the past's spoken, unspoken and even sepulchral presence reinforce the thrust of Dickson's article on the *dit* and the *non-dit* in Corneille.

'*Bérénice*: tragedy or anti-tragedy?' (Richard Parish) calls into question the accepted interpretation of cathartic release at the end of the play. Parish stresses the paradox that Bérénice's race and sex modify the genre of the play: Bérénice's final decision to live subverts the traditional Roman ethic of 'gloire'. Instead of three exemplary suicides, Parish posits a trio of exemplary renunciations, the anti-'glorieux' option instigated by a foreign queen. Both play and preface give the lie to Corneille's theory and dramatic achievement: '*Bérénice* is an anti-tragedy [because behind claims of orthodoxy] is hidden an unambiguous statement of theatrical, political, and indeed sexual iconoclasm'. As in Cronk's reappraisal of *Les Amants magnifiques*, Parish's reading encourages a radical, critical refocussing of the theatrical aims of Racine as expressed in the *Préface* and embodied in the play.

In revisiting both traditional and new critical directives on the staging of *Phèdre*, James Supple reassesses the play *qua* script ('Phèdre's Guilt: a theatrical reading'). Is Phèdre a 'marionnette sacrée' for whom the goddess of love is no more than a pretext to justify her actions? Should we place an actual statue of Venus on stage to receive Phèdre's prayer or should we merely dim the lighting to suggest the presence of a malevolent deity? By concentrating on the theatrical experience, Supple leaves us with the tantalising question: 'Perhaps the ultimate tragedy of Phèdre is that she just fails to free herself of the impurities from which she would, indeed, have dearly loved to escape. Even in death, she is "ni tout à fait coupable, ni tout à fait innocente" '.

After demythologising hero, *fourbe*, ascetic, and tragic heroine, the conference proceeded to demythologise the critic and teacher ('Seventeenth-century French studies: an appraisal'). How do we, without modish distortion, make seventeenth-century works relevant to the 1990s? How do we resuscitate authors who have over the last ten to twenty years been relegated to the mausoleum? In 1992, students appear to be choosing the enticing 'chemins de la liberté' as opposed to the austere 'chemins de la méthode'! However, if the critic can find ever-increasing charm in giving new directions to familiar landmarks, surely the teacher (of whatever *orientation*) can equally re-create and re-present the period's distinctive achievement?

Elizabeth Moles and Noël Peacock

La Fontaine's Fable II, 4
and
French Classicism

BY

CHRISTOPHER SMITH

UNIVERSITY OF EAST ANGLIA

1   Humiles laborant ubi potentes dissident.
Rana e palude pugnam taurorum intuens
'Heu, quanta nobis instat pernicies' ait.
interrogata ab alia cur hoc diceret,
5   de principatu cum illi certarent gregis
longeque ab ipsis degerent uitam boues:
'Sit statio separata ac diuersum genus;
expulsus regno nemoris qui profugerit,
paludis in secreta ueniet latibula,
10   et proculcatas obteret duro pede.
ita caput ad nostrum furor illorum pertinet'. (Phaedrus, I, 30)

LES DEUX TAUREAUX ET UNE GRENOUILLE

1   Deux Taureaux combattaient à qui posséderait
        Une Génisse avec l'empire.
        Une Grenouille en soupirait.
        Qu'avez-vous? se mit à lui dire
5   Quelqu'un du peuple croassant.
        —Et ne voyez-vous pas, dit-elle,
        Que la fin de cette querelle
Sera l'exil de l'un; que l'autre, le chassant,
Le fera renoncer aux campagnes fleuries?
10   Il ne régnera plus sur l'herbe des prairies,
Viendra dans nos marais régner sur les roseaux,
Et nous foulant aux pieds jusques au fond des eaux,
Tantôt l'une, et puis l'autre, il faudra qu'on pâtisse
Du combat qu'a causé Madame la Génisse.

15   Cette crainte était de bon sens.
          L'un des Taureaux en leur demeure
          S'alla cacher à leur dépens:
          Il en écrasait vingt par heure.
          Hélas! on voit que de tout temps
20   Les petits ont pâti des sottises des grands. (La Fontaine, II, 4)

A comparison of Phaedrus's text[1] with the fable that La Fontaine[2] based
upon it will serve to bring into focus a consideration of primordial
importance about French Classicism.[3] The contrast will serve to
highlight the dependency of French seventeenth-century culture upon its
classical heritage. Although this dependency has long been accepted as
an established fact, our sense of pleasure in the felicity of its aesthetic
consequences will be kindled afresh. It is worth first rehearsing the
reasons why we should retain a sense of surprise that ancient classical
sources retained their hold upon the imagination of the poets of the
period.

   In the movement *ad fontes* during the Renaissance, the return of the
arts generally to ancient sources, which had in fact always been
subjacent to practice earlier too, is readily comprehensible within a
context of a sense of inferiority that applied no less to scientific and
technological matters than to cultural issues. This was doubtless
reinforced by a religious tradition, which likewise was prone to look
back with veneration to what its leaders regarded as superior primitive
times in an age when the label 'primitive' carried no pejorative
implications. But radical changes set in,[4] and it is not difficult to agree
with Elizabeth Eisenstein that the printing press was instrumental in the
process. This handmaiden of the Renaissance furnished incontrovertible
documentation on the limitations of what had been rediscovered, and,

---

[1] Phaedri, *Fabulae Aesopiae*, ed. J.P. Postgate (Oxford, 1920).

[2] La Fontaine, *Fables*, Livres I-VI, ed. J.-P. Collinet (Paris, 1974), p. 87. See also the edition by
M. Fumaroli, *Fables*, I (Paris, 1985), and notably his excellent introduction (pp. 14-28) on the
rhetorical background of the genre.

[3] There is some confusion over terminology in English, as is shown by W.D. Howarth's article
'Neo-Classicism in France : A Reassessment', *Studies in the French Eighteenth Century presented to
John Lough*, ed. D.J. Mossop, G.E. Rodmell and D.B. Wilson (Durham, 1978), pp. 92-107 (see
especially the opening pages). Opting for 'French Classicism', while indicating clearly which country's
culture is under discussion, also has the advantage of avoiding any possible confusion with that very
self-conscious return to Antiquity in the late eighteenth and early nineteenth century which is, in large
measure, a rejection of much that constitutes French Classicism as encountered in the seventeenth
century.

[4] As is implied, of course, by the very title of C.S. Lewis's *The Discarded Image* (Cambridge,
1964).

more pertinently, diffused awareness of its precariousness to a wider readership on an unprecedented scale.[5] New worlds knocked Ptolemaic geography out of shape,[6] just as Galileo untuned classical astronomy, at a time when religious reform, for all its apparently impeccable Humanistic appeal to the early texts, was conspicuously failing to usher in obvious improvement,[7] and the states of Europe were in turmoil. All around them, men were confronted with evidence of technological advance that left Antiquity behind, from the design of the caravels that crossed the Atlantic to the printing presses that related their journeys. Gun powder consigned Roman battle tactics to history, and Harvey swept ancient physiology off its feet.[8] Inflation, it is suggested, added to uncertainty about values generally,[9] and, in France as elsewhere, the ancient customary structures of the state were being swept away and replaced by the new monarchies.[10]

In philosophy, the ancient verities were fast being eroded and, aided by fresh investigation of St Augustine, belief in human dignity became less and less fashionable. All these factors combined to contribute to a sense that all was flux in the intellectual climate; the Ancients lost their unimpeachable authority, and the conviction grew that progress would not be guaranteed by a systematic return to the past. The text that is perhaps the most striking witness to a change, which cannot, of course, be precisely dated or, even less, be attributed to one thinker, is Francis Bacon's *Advancement of Learning*.[11] The provocative title affords crisp comment on the Herculean intellectual labours that had characterized the previous century and a half. Bacon's programme suggests a systematic recension of what Antiquity had to offer, precisely in order to determine what remained to be discovered, not by further recourse to the old texts, but rather by means of a different method, namely the scientific investigation of nature by the inductive method.[12]

All this points up an intriguing truth which perhaps does not always attract the attention it deserves: namely, that French Classicism, far

---

[5] E. Eisenstein, *The Printing Press as an Agent of Change*, 2 vols (Cambridge, 1979).

[6] J.H. Parry, *The Age of Reconnaissance* (London, 1963).

[7] O. Chadwick, *The Reformation* (Harmondsworth, 1964). The consequences of the return to the Greek New Testament revealed that this essentially Humanistic endeavour could well be most damaging.

[8] W. Harvey, *The Circulation of the Blood*, trans. K.J. Franklin (London, 1963).

[9] *The Fontana Economic History of Europe: The Sixteenth and Seventeenth Centuries*, ed. Carlo M. Cipolla (Geneva, 1974).

[10] H.G. Koenigsberger and George Mosse, *Europe in the Sixteenth Century* (London, 1972).

[11] Francis Bacon, *The Advancement of Learning*, The World's Classics, No. 93 (London, 1906).

[12] Eisenstein, II, passim.

from occupying a natural place in the context of an all-embracing Humanist endeavour, must be seen as a cultural force in the Early Modern period, at a time when its respect for, and devotion to the theory and practice of its Greek and Roman forbears cannot but be regarded as exceptional within the intellectual framework of its time. Perhaps some analogies with Counter-Reformation Catholicism can be found, though only at the cost of denying some strikingly novel elements in the seventeenth-century Church, but generally French Classicism has to be regarded as a far less obviously appropriate response to the spirit of age than its rival, the inchoate Baroque movement.[13] Aesthetic factors, though plainly they may have been involved to some degree, seem unlikely to be the prime consideration here. Though, later on, writers and critics make of *raison* the prime buttress of the French Classical manner, especially in the theatre,[14] their debate might as easily be turned on its head as taken at face value. What seems still to count is authority, reinforced by the prestige of accredited tradition, and the acceptance of it, in a period when in other spheres it was being questioned, and even downright rejected, would suggest that it provided certainty in an age of doubt, a comfortable and consoling sense of familiarity in a time of distressing change. In France this was paralleled by the emergence of political authoritarianism. The harnessing of the Classical manner to the enhancement of the prestige of the crown was to be one of the constants in cultural policy throughout the seventeenth century and indeed beyond.[15]

Yet when French seventeenth-century writers reassert the authority of Antiquity, they do so, as La Fontaine's *Préface* demonstrates, in ways that are different from those encountered during the Renaissance. First, there is the passage familiar to all: 'aujourd'hui [...] on veut de la nouveauté et de la gaieté'. It is worth insisting on the first of these desiderata. For, if La Fontaine's observation is just, then the times might well, as has already been suggested, hardly have been propitious for a classicizing enterprise, and a public that demanded both innovation and also *divertissement* might be thought not to be likely to be predisposed to respond to classical qualities generally. Second, we may note La Fontaine's *honnête* disclaimer of being a pioneer in

---

[13] W. Floeck, *Die Literaturästhetik der französischen Barock*, Studienreihe Romania, No. 4 (Berlin, 1979), pp. 17-71.

[14] For a classic statement, see Racine's *Discours prononcé à l'Académie française à la réception de M. [Thomas] de Corneille*, in *Œuvres complètes*, ed. R. Picard, 2 vols, Bibliothèque de la Pléiade (Paris, 1960-64), 344-50.

[15] E. Caldicott, 'Richelieu and the Arts', *Richelieu and his Age*, ed. J. Bergin and L. Brockliss (Oxford, 1992), pp. 203-36.

scholarship.[16] He carries his learning lightly, as well he might, in view of the fact that the fables were indeed 'sues de tout le monde' in a variety of earlier versions,[17] but the change in attitude from boastful Renaissance prefaces and liminary verses is striking.[18] What was once the proud preserve of scholars has now become the common coin of cultural intercourse in the *salon*. Just as regular tragedy had at length found its way out of the colleges, and now offered itself to the critical gaze of adults in the public theatres,[19] so too the fable in La Fontaine's hands, escaped from the school room to become reading for adults. The transition, however, is accomplished in yet another way that is characteristic of French Classicism. La Fontaine still offers a text for the young Dauphin to enjoy and think about, but for those capable of looking further, there was more besides. Following a policy which is very characteristic of French Classicism, an ancient form is taken over and adapted, but not stretched too far beyond its normal limits, and certainly not exploded.[20] An alert reader, well aware of both generic norms and paradigmatic models, would, we may be sure, appreciate the delicate interplay between the satisfying of expectations and the surpassing of them.

One aspect of this lies in the choice and use of language which La Fontaine comments on specifically in his *Préface*. He makes due obeisance to 'l'élégance' and 'l'extrême brèveté' of Phaedrus, lauding his style by saying it is comparable with that of Terence, and admiringly commenting that 'la simplicité est magnifique chez ces grands hommes'. The qualities of Phaedrus are, he says, 'au-dessus de ma portée', and he goes on to explain that he who lacked 'les perfections du langage comme ils les ont eues' could not hope to equal the two Latin authors in simple, elegant concision. His response to this realization is, however, different from what it would have been in the sixteenth century. Du Bellay's view was that the French language had to be consciously developed in order to make it capable of answering the challenge of imitating the various styles used by the ancient authors.[21] La Fontaine has registered these differences, however, and then, without more ado, he informs his

---

[16] See ed. cit., p. 28.

[17] See ibid., p. 27, and on the background, B. Tieman, *Fabel und Emblem* (München, 1974), pp. 21-39; M.-O. Sweetser, *La Fontaine*, TWAS No. 788 (Boston, 1987), pp. 48-51.

[18] Ronsard's 'Dithyrambes à la pompe du bouc de D. Jodelle', *Œuvres complètes*, ed. G. Cohen, Bibliothèque de la Pléiade, 2 vols (Paris, 1966), II, pp. 764-73, offer a striking extreme example of the praise meted out to those who adopted the classical manner.

[19] R. Lebègue, *La Tragédie française de la Renaissance* (Bruxelles, 1944).

[20] A similar point might, of course, be made about Bossuet's *Oraisons funèbres*.

[21] J. Du Bellay, *Déffense et illustration de la langue françoise*, ed. H. Chamard (Paris, 1948).

readers that he will therefore adopt a different strategy. He does, admittedly, adduce a classical precedent—Quintillian—for what he intends to do, but his resolve to create a different art form because of a qualitative gap between Latin and French bespeaks a linguistic self-confidence and, indeed, self-sufficiency which would not have been met with three generations sooner. It is true that La Fontaine's own idiom, with its readiness to exploit the riches of a vocabulary reaching back to Marot and Rabelais, is more varied than that of many of his contemporaries, but in his rejection of any notion that French stands in a client relationship to the ancient languages, he clearly belongs to the seventeenth century.

Obedient to the universal classical doctrine (which has particular pertinence for the fable), that in art *l'agréable* must serve the cause of inculcating the good, La Fontaine bids us concentrate on the lessons to be learned from his fables. Yet in the treatment of the moral in 'Les Deux Taureaux et une grenouille', we may see an avoidance of the dangers of magisterial, platitudinous moralizing in favour of a presentation which is more likely to hold attention, and arguably even to make a greater impact by engaging the readers or listeners.[22] Whether young or old, they were, as La Fontaine knew quite as well as did Pascal, more likely to be persuaded by arguments which they at least felt they had discovered for themselves. For Phaedrus, it was a matter of course to place the moral, for clarity's sake, at the head of the fable, and his statement of it is in fact somewhat flat. 'Humiles' and 'potentes' do not stand in clear-cut diametric opposition, and the two verbs lack force. La Fontaine is altogether more sophisticated: first, relating the story from which we are initially encouraged to draw our own conclusions. 'Heu' comes early in the Latin fable and is not reinforced; La Fontaine, on the other hand, gives us 'soupirait' (l. 3) early, then strengthens its impact with 'Hélas!' in the penultimate line after the intelligent expectation of disaster has been fulfilled. In the final line ('Les petits ont pâti des sottises des grands') his use of the perfect tense hints at the possibility of future escape from the dire inevitability of oppression of the weak by the strong, whereas Phaedrus denies even this fragile possibility by employing a present which conveys a verity all the more painful for being eternal. 'Petits' and 'grands' offer a vivid juxtaposition, and, most strikingly, the Latin 'furor', which in the seventeenth-century context might carry positive heroic overtones of

---

[22] P. Dumonceaux draws attention to the importance of the reading aloud of literary texts in 'La Lecture à haute voix des œuvres littéraires au XVIIème siècle: modalités et valeurs', *La Voix au XVIIème siècle, Littératures classiques* (1990), 177-85.

military triumph for the French, is replaced by the savagely judgemental 'sottises' in a line where 'pâtir' is repeated for the second time (ll. 13-20).

The complications of the fable emerge yet more strongly when La Fontaine clarifies the issues. No doubt in France in the seventeenth century, no less than in ancient times, everybody knew perfectly well what was involved when bulls fought 'de principatu [...] gregis' (l. 5), yet there is an undeniable increase in interest when the rather coy abstraction is replaced by a reference, not to bulls in general, but to a pair of them fighting to determine 'qui posséderait / Une Génisse' (ll. 1-2), especially since the attractive heifer stands in an emphatic position at the head of the second line. In other words, La Fontaine, like the authors of French classical tragedies who, in Boileau's view,[23] might go too far in this direction, is conforming to the French classical strategy of bringing out the sexual side of the situation that is being explored. This dimension is further emphasized when La Fontaine deftly contrives to suggest sexes for the frogs who discuss the scene. Phaedrus was content to let grammatical genders run their course ('interrogata ab alia' (l. 4)), but by employing the mock-heroic periphrasis 'quelqu'un du peuple croassant' (l. 5) and then, later on, by emphasizing their unison in disapproval 'Tantôt l'une, et puis l'autre' (l. 13) La Fontaine is able to hint at a stupidity in males, whether bulls or frogs, which contrasts with the greater wisdom of females who, though debarred by sex from martial activity and allowed only to look on, are able to judge events coolly. Sexual roles are further stressed when La Fontaine deletes 'furor illorum' and inserts: 'Du combat qu'a causé madame la génisse' (l. 14). The mute *e* puts ironic stress on the faintly ridiculous courtesy title by holding back the line, which allows us a moment to consider likely collocations, and to build up expectations which are promptly revealed to be mistaken. At one level all this can be taken as no more than laconically graphic homely detail, but it is surely true that, like his contemporaries, La Fontaine finds it appropriate to stress the interplay between the sexes when reshaping his topic.

If such details add life to the familiar tale, so too does a good deal of what may readily be interpreted as alert contemporary comment within the context of the ancient fable. Is there not, one cannot but ask, after taking into account the use of such potentially loaded words as 'l'empire', and 'régner', also some specific allusion in granting the heifer the title 'madame' in an era when dynastic considerations were so important in the formulation of French foreign policy? By the same

---

[23] Boileau, *Art poétique*, ed. J.-C. Lambert and F. Mizrachi (Paris, 1966), III, 94-104.

token, the conflict that will end by one of the parties involved taking refuge in marshland, to the detriment of the wretched, humble inhabitants, cannot but have struck a chord in a period when France was regularly engaged in war in the Low Countries. Turenne's conquest of Flanders in the summer of 1667, in particular provoked the formation of an anti-French triple alliance. Once we have become sensitized to possible political overtones, it is hard to resist the temptation of giving a specific twist to the stigmatized 'les grands' of the last line.

If La Fontaine's attitude towards public affairs in seventeenth-century France and, no less pertinently, his oblique presentation of it has much in common with what we find in the works of many of his French contemporaries, he also shares much with them in his presentation of a bleak view of humanity. Humble folk are at the mercy of their superiors who are anything but embodiments of virtue or wisdom. The comparisons with animals that are implicit in fable writing generally are far from flattering, the more so as human action here is seen as nothing more admirable than the instinctive behaviour of brute beasts. It is true that a similar inference might be drawn from Phaedrus's work, but he is operating according to the 'orientation ancienne' by inculcating responses deemed appropriate to slaves in a hierarchical society.[24] What Phaedrus suggests amounts essentially to disabused resignation unalloyed by the allurements of fallacious hopes. The French scene which La Fontaine surveys in the mid-seventeenth century is no more gratifying than the ancient world to which Phaedrus bears witness, and there is no trace of the attitudes that have been warrant enough for identifying in the French Renaissance a 'dignitas hominis' theme.[25] Whether in human relationships, class conflict or international affairs, 'Les Deux Taureaux et une grenouille' finds much that is displeasing, and, of course, the fable's conclusions are by no means unique in French classical literature. Both in the view of mankind transmitted most strikingly by Pascal and by the moralists,[26] and in the picture of society and of the state as presented most memorably by La Bruyère, there is evidence of a profound pessimism which later historians have had no difficulty in showing to be entirely justified. Richelieu and Louis XIV took great pains to glorify the periods when they governed France.[27] Their

---

[24] Aesop was, of course, a slave, and Phaedrus a freedman, but the view that for mankind wisdom lay in accepting subservience was widespread in antiquity.

[25] L. Sozzi, 'La "dignitas hominis" thème dans la littérature française de la Renaissance', *Humanism in France*, ed. A.H.T. Levi (Manchester, 1970), pp. 176-98.

[26] A. Krailsheimer's choice of title, *Studies in Self-Interest* (Oxford, 1962), eloquently sums up the issue.

[27] Caldicott, art. cit. and P. Burke, *The Fabrication of Louis XIV* (New Haven, 1992).

realization that the unembroidered truth could not but tarnish their reputations must have been a dominant motive for their taking such pains to magnify their 'gloire'. One aspect of the French Classicism of La Fontaine resides, then, in his reflection, through a form and by means of a base text borrowed from antiquity, of the pessimism about humanity that was typical of his time. Moreover, there is also a conviction, which he shares with other French writers of the age, that the state, far from offering solutions to problems, was in fact exacerbating them by displaying on the grandest scale man's invincible tendency toward vanity, folly and cruelty.

In his alert appreciation of man's condition, which was made worse by seventeenth-century circumstance, La Fontaine reveals himself to be a writer of his time. He is less willing than Phaedrus to conceal complaint beneath a blanket of sage resignation, but he stops well short of loud protest. Like Molière, who, in Jean Anouilh's words, 'dans un moule de comédie raisonnable a écrit le théâtre le plus noir de la littérature de tous les temps',[28] and then turned from it to wrap things up in farcical action and comic conclusions, La Fontaine makes his observations with clinical perceptiveness and then takes refuge in wit, irony and humour. The dedication of the first six books of the *Fables* to the Dauphin is an emblem of La Fontaine's close relationship with, and dependency on, the system of which he was a discerning critic. Given the experience of Foucquet, the King's favours could, as he well knew, be withdrawn on a whim. Whether consciously or not, he had schooled himself not to protest too loudly at such a flagrant miscarriage of justice at a period when the King, given his view of humanity, certainly could not be expected to listen. There was an alternative for writers who could not bear such constraints on their freedom of expression, but the political motives of those who opted to emigrate to the Low Countries were generally underpinned by religious conviction too.[29] For La Fontaine, as for other writers of the French classical canon, exile involving departure from metropolitan France and the drying up of patronage was too high a price to pay. French Classicism is the literature of *la cour et la ville*, contrasting in this respect with the French literature of the Enlightenment, virtually all the major works of which were published outside the boundaries of the kingdom.

In this review of French classical traits in La Fontaine, attention has been focused on his relatively free, yet, as we have seen, not unfaithful

---

[28] Quoted by M. Descotes in *Molière et sa fortune littéraire* (Saint-Médard-en-Jalles, 1970), p. 151.

[29] Eisenstein, *Grub Street Abroad: Aspects of the French Cosmopolitan Press from the Age of Louis XIV to the French Revolution* (Oxford, 1992).

imitation of an ancient text which is assumed to be familiar to all, in
order to facilitate, with the aid of techniques tried and honed by his
contemporaries, the aesthetic expression of a view of man's position in
society and in the state which they also shared. What is perhaps missing
is his contemporaries' emphasis on the important qualities of balance
and harmony in achieving a rounded picture of man's place in the
world. Certainly there is a nicely calculated interplay between
Phaedrus's text and La Fontaine's and, as always, an admirably judged
economy of means in the telling of the vivid miniature narrative and in
the drawing of the moral. But, while appreciating these qualities, we
readers can sense a certain subterranean tension in our poet. The ancient
form is employed, first, to fulfil its ostensible function of charmingly
imparting to the young Dauphin unexceptionable moral instruction and,
next, to hand on to a more mature public not only the pleasures of
seeing the fable so adroitly manipulated in a faux-naïf fashion, but also
the challenge of responding to the reinterpretation of the traditional
model in the light of contemporary circumstances. There is likewise a
charge of tension in La Fontaine's juxtaposition of obvious levity with a
bleakness of outlook about the unsatisfactory state of affairs in
seventeenth-century France which it was not politic to express more
openly. As in Molière's comedies and Racine's tragedies, an energy
courses beneath the surface of La Fontaine's fables which is barely held
in check by the constraints of form and propriety.

'Paysage héroïque': seventeenth-century and more recent perceptions of Poussin's landscapes[1]

BY

CLAIRE PACE

UNIVERSITY OF GLASGOW

I: 'Une espèce de création'

In artistic theory in seventeenth-century France, the category of landscape painting ranked low in the hierarchy of 'genres', since this theory derived largely from Italian art-historical writings of the late sixteenth and early seventeenth centuries, with their pronounced humanistic bias. According to these treatises, the highest kind of painting was 'history painting', the depiction of noble human actions (or the conflict of human passions), while the representation of inanimate nature was allotted a lower rank, below that of portraiture. In part, this was a consequence of the desire to elevate the art of painting to the level of that of poetry, as one of the liberal arts; history painting was held to be more intellectual, and was associated with 'disegno', the art of design, while the lesser genres, especially landscape, were associated with practice rather than theory, and with colour rather than design. It was also asserted by hostile critics that such representations presented no challenge to the artist's imagination, but merely involved literal copying of the external world.[2]

[1] Richard Verdi has given a full account of the 'critical fortunes' of Poussin's paintings (including landscapes) in his unpublished doctoral thesis, 'Poussin's Critical Fortune: the study of the Artist and the Criticism of his Works from c. 1690 to c. 1830' (University of London, 1976). He has paid special attention to the *Deluge* and *Shepherds in Arcadia*, and I have therefore not dealt with the extensive material relating to these works. I have, however, thought it worth expanding on some of the points touched on in his thesis, in particular the 17th-century critical context, notably the writings of Félibien and De Piles regarding landscape in general.

[2] The views of leading 16th- and 17th-century Italian critics are summarized in M. Lagerlof, *Ideal Landscape* (New Haven and London, 1990), esp. pp. 27.

André Félibien's attitude to this question was more complex than is often allowed. The Préface to the *Conférences* of the Académie Royale (written in his official role as *historiographe*) has often been cited as representative of this rather rigid view, whereby landscape ranks below allegory and history painting; to achieve 'cette haute perfection de l'art [...], il faut représenter de grandes actions comme les Historiens, ou des sujets agréables comme les Poètes; & montant encore plus haut, il faut par des compositions allégoriques, sçavoir couvrir sous le voile de fable les vertus des grands hommes & les mystères les plus relevez [...]'. However, Félibien does allow that 'celui qui fait parfaitement des paysages est au-dessus d'un autre qui ne fait que des fruits, des fleurs, ou des coquilles [...]'.[3]

A similar attitude prevails in Félibien's assertion, in his ninth *Entretien*, that painters should be ranked according to their talent, distinguishing between 'ceux qui travaillent à l'histoire, d'avec ceux qui ne font que des portraits, ou des Batailles, ou des Paysages, ou des animaux, ou des fleurs, ou des fruits [...]'.[4]

However, the severity of this judgement is again qualified in his recognition of the variety of talents in the same *Entretien*:

> ... dans la peinture on loue avec justice, ceux qui ont parfaitement réussi à faire des paysages, des fleurs, des fruits & des animaux, quand leur génie n'a pas été capable de plus grands sujets [...].[5]

Such 'low' subjects might be justified by 'le beau choix', which was one of the crucial points whereby the painting of landscape was given greater dignity, as involving the artist's judgement and powers of selection.

In his discussion of individual artists, also, Félibien shows himself receptive and sympathetic to landscape. This is particularly evident, as we shall see, in his consideration of Poussin's landscapes, but may be seen also in his remarks on other artists, notably Titian (referring to a painting in his own collection). He praises above all Titian's mastery of colour, as well as the 'beau choix des arbres' and grouping of light and shade, and singles out the way the artist handles foliage 'légèrement & avec esprit'.[6]

---

[3] Félibien, Preface to *Conférences de l'Académie Royale de Peinture* (1667; reprinted in the 1725 edition of the *Entretiens* and later by Farnborough, 1967); this passage is cited by Lagerlof, op. cit., n. 17 to ch. 4.

[4] Félibien, *Entretiens sur la vie et les ouvrages des plus excellens peintres anciens et modernes*, 4 vols. (1666-1668; ed. Trévoux, 1725); reprinted by Farnborough (1967). References here are to the 1725 edition.

[5] Ibid., p. 166.

[6] *Entretien*, V, p. 102.

Such a detailed analysis springs from a sympathetic response to landscape, and indeed Félibien avows his liking for the genre when referring to Du Fresnoy's copies of Titian (attributing his own admiration for the Venetian artist to the influence of Poussin).[7] But the severity of tone recurs in Félibien's warning that artists should not be beguiled by the charms of landscape, however beautiful, since the official view was that only the human figures should have the artist's full attention, and should claim precedence.[8]

This ambiguity is also present in statements by other writers who, while decrying the claims of landscape in relation to history painting, recognize the supremacy of Titian in this category. Thus Du Fresnoy (who, as we have seen, copied Titian's paintings) declared in 1678: 'Personne n'a jamais fait le Paysage de si grande Maniere, de si bonne condition, ny qui fist voir tant de vérité [...]'.[9] Elsewhere, Du Fresnoy asserts of Titian that '[...] il n'y a point encore eu personne qui aye fait le paysage de si grande maniere ny si bien colorié comme luy.'[10]

With the growing strength of the Académie Royale de Peinture, the denigration of landscape and other 'lesser' categories becomes even more emphatic. For instance, Henri Testelin, in the fifth of the 'Tables' included in his *Sentimens* of 1680, largely ignores landscape except as a background for historical scenes[11] — although he does make an interesting distinction between 'inhabited' and 'uninhabited' landscapes which may perhaps parallel Roger de Piles's pairing of 'héroïque' and 'champêtre'.[12] The published *Conférences* of the Académie, as has been noted, include only two devoted to landscape, or to paintings where landscape is a predominant feature (shorter than the lectures devoted to history painting): on Poussin's *Deluge* and his *Ruth and Boaz* (from the *Seasons*).

Nevertheless, despite academic disdain, the category of landscape had its adherents in theory, as well as increasing popularity in practice, and was established in the seventeenth century as an independent category for the first time. Whether explicitly or implicitly, landscape might be elevated in a number of ways: by the inclusion of classical themes

---

[7] Ibid.

[8] Ibid.

[9] C.A. du Fresnoy, 'Sentimens sur les ouvrages des principaux et meilleurs Peintres des derniers siècles', in *L'Art de peinture* (1678), pp. 265-6.

[10] J. Thuillier (ed.), 'Les "Observations de la Peinture" de Du Fresnoy', in *Walter Friedlaender zum 90 Geburstag* (Berlin, 1965), pp. 193 ff., lines 236 ff.

[11] H. Testelin, *Sentimens des plus habiles peintres* (1680), 1696 ed., p. 29.

[12] Testelin's reference to landscape occurs in his fifth 'table', on 'Ordonnance', under the heading of 'Disposition' (cf. Verdi, 'Poussin's Critical Fortunes', p. 198).

(where the landscape setting might be considered to mirror or enhance
the significance of such themes); by the selection of the most beautiful
parts of a particular scene to form an 'ideal' nature (deriving from the
precepts of Italian writers, notably Agucchi and Bellori).[13] The
landscapes of Carracci and Domenichino, and even more those of
Lorrain and Poussin, were held to embody such an ideal, and were
associated with the notion of a Virgilian Golden Age.[14]

Dignity was also given to the category of landscape by an appeal to
the authority of classical precedents, as recounted in the writings of
Pliny, or in Junius' *De Pictura veterum* of 1637 which was widely read
throughout Europe in the seventeenth century.[15] Most important, as
Gombrich has shown, is Vitruvius's division of theatrical scenery into
three types—a division taken up by Serlio in his description of the
'tragic', 'comic' and 'satyric' scenes.[16] The links between the stage and
the composition of 'ideal' landscape have been shown to be close,[17] and
would continue to be of importance to the French followers of Claude
and Poussin. Apart from such compositional factors as the framing trees
or buildings in such landscapes, resembling the 'wings' of baroque stage
design, the underlying concept of the landscape as a fitting 'setting' for
the drama of human emotion of the protagonists depicted is of
fundamental importance.

Vitruvius's distinction of three types of stage scenery may underlie
the analysis of de Piles, who, in his *Cours de peinture*, was the first
important French critic to devote a section of his treatise to landscape,
thereby subverting the traditional hierarchy of genres.[18] As a
'Rubéniste' par excellence, and advocate of 'le coloris' in the debate
which preoccupied the Académie,[19] de Piles would be predisposed to an
appreciation of landscape—and of more naturalistic as well as 'ideal'

[13] For G.B. Agucchi, *Trattato*, see D. Mahon, *Studies in 17th-century Art and Theory* (London, 1947). Cf. C. Whitfield, 'A Programme for Erminia and the Shepherds by G.B. Agucchi', *Storia dell'arte* (1973). G.P. Bellori's *Idea* was printed as a preface to his *Vite de' pittori, scultori ed architetti moderni* of 1672; cf. Lagerlof, op. cit., pp. 189-93.

[14] Cf. for instance Lagerlof, op. cit., passim, esp. pp. 7 ff.

[15] Franciscus Junius the Younger was Librarian to the Earl of Arundel. His *De Pictura Veterum* was published in 1637; his English version, *The Painting of the Ancients*, in 1638.

[16] Vitruvius, *De Architettura*, Lib.V., chs. 6, 8; Serlio, *L'Architettura*, Book 2, 154-5; cf. E.H. Gombrich, 'Renaissance Artistic Theory and the Development of Landscape Painting', *Gazette des Beaux-Arts*, 41 (1953); rept. (as 'The Renaissance Theory of Art and the Rise of Landscape') in *Norm and Form* (London, 1966).

[17] Cf. esp. Lagerlof, op. cit., pp. 11-12, and 95 ff.

[18] R. de Piles, *Cours de peinture par principes* (Paris, 1708); for the chapter on 'Le Paisage', cf. pp. 200 ff. See also Verdi, op. cit.

[19] On this debate, see esp. B. Teyssèdre, *Roger de Piles et le débat sur le coloris* (Paris, 1957).

types of landscape. In his justification of the genre, de Piles resorts to the traditional image of the artist as creator, implying an analogy with divine Creation; according to this criterion, the landscape painter ranks above all others: 'Ainsi la Peinture, qui est une espece de création, l'est encore plus particulièrement à l'égard du paysage.'[20]

De Piles is catholic in his appreciation of a wide variety of different kinds of landscape:

> Entre tous les plaisirs que les différens talens de la Peinture procurent pour ceux qui les exercent, celui de faire du Paysage me paraît le plus sensible, & le plus commode; car dans la grande variété dont il est susceptible, le Peintre a plus d'occasions que dans tous les autres genres de cet Art de se contenter dans le choix des objets [...] Enfin il est le Maître de disposer de tout ce qui se voit sur la terre, sur les eaux, & dans les airs: parce que de tous les productions de l'Art & de la Nature, il n'y en a une qui ne puisse entrer dans la composition de ses Tableaux [...][21]

De Piles's analogy with divine creation occurs again in his *Idée du peintre parfait*, where he makes the highest claim for the category of landscape painting as epitomising, as it were, all other kinds, and moreover empowering the artist to exercise his powers of selection, thus creating order out of chaos:[22]

> Si la Peinture est une espèce de creation, elle en donne des marques encore plus sensibles dans les Tableaux de Paysages, que dans les autres. On y voit plus généralement la Nature sortie de son cahos, & les Elemens plus débrouillez [...]. Et comme ce genre de Peinture contient en raccourci tous les autres, le Peintre qui l'exerce, doit avoir une connaissance universelle des parties de son Art [...].

In the *Cours*, de Piles goes on to make the celebrated distinction between 'héroïque' and 'champêtre', or pastoral, landscapes — explicitly citing Poussin as the exemplar of the former category and the Flemish artist Foucquier as that of the latter. Although the passage is familiar, it is worth quoting part of it here, because — as has been recognized — the passage identifies the main currents in seventeenth-century French landscape art in a way that remains valid.[23] He distinguishes two essential styles, of which others may be 'un mélange', 'le style héroïque' and 'le style pastoral ou champêtre':

---

[20] De Piles, *Cours*, p. 201.

[21] Loc. cit.

[22] De Piles, *Idée du peintre parfait*, ptd. in *Abrégé de la vie et des œuvres des plus célèbres peintres* (Paris, 1715); also, as by Félibien, in the 1725 edition of the *Entretiens*; cf. Ch. XVII, 'Du paisage'.

[23] As noted by M. Kitson in 'The Seventeenth Century', in exhibition catalogue, *Claude to Corot* (New York, Colnaghi, 1990), pp. 11 ff. Cf. de Piles, *Cours*, pp. 201-02.

> Le style Héroïque est une composition d'objets qui dans leur genre tirent de l'Art & de la Nature ce que l'un & l'autre peuvent produire de grand & d'extraordinaire. Les sites en sont tout agréables & tout surprenans: les fabriques n'y sont que temples, que pyramides, que sépulcres antiques, qu'autels consacrés aux divinités, que maisons de plaisance d'une régulière architecture, & si la Nature n'y est pas exprimée comme le hazard nous le fait voir tous les jours, elle y est du moins représentée comme on s'imagine qu'elle devroit être. Ce style est une agréable illusion & une espece d'enchantement quand il part d'un beau génie & d'un bon esprit, comme étoit celui du Poussin.

De Piles warns, however, of the difficulties inherent in attempting this style for those without requisite talent, who risk becoming 'puérile'. He defines 'le style champêtre' as 'une représentation des Pais qui paroissent bien moins cultivés qu'abandonnés à la bizarerie de la seule Nature. Elle s'y fait voir toute simple, sans fard, & sans artifice [...]'. In the 'champêtre' style, greater variety of sites is allowed: sometimes extensive, sometimes 'sauvages [...] pour servir de retraite aux Solitaires, & de sureté aux animaux sauvages'.

In his substantial chapter on landscape, de Piles discusses various aspects such as 'les sites'; it is, none the less, the human theme which is seen as determining the 'character' of the scene as a whole.[24] So even for de Piles it is the human protagonists who dominate the composition—though they need not, in his view, be drawn from classical or biblical narrative, in order to give the landscape its 'heroic' quality, but may be 'de simples figures passageres'. He recognizes that an artist may introduce figures which accord with his particular style, 'comme a fait Poussin dans son Héroïque, & Foucquier dans son Champêtre avec toute la vraisemblance & la grace possible.' Notably de Piles acknowledges that figures may be passive, contemplative, without detracting from the worth of the composition.

It is significant that de Piles singles out 'vraisemblance' as one of the qualities he admires, for it is lifelike verisimilitude—a matter for criticism with other writers—that now becomes one of the justifications of landscape. Another quality, formerly criticized, that is now seen as one of the causes of the appeal of landscape, is that of its freedom from rules, its inherently subversive quality. Just as the eye has liberty to roam over an extensive prospect, so the painter of landscape has greater licence than the artist concerned with biblical or mythological subject-matter. This is linked with the psychological effect of the contemplation

---

[24] Ibid, pp. 228 ff.

of landscape, singled out by its advocates, bringing rest and refreshment to the spirit of the spectator.[25]

II: Poussin: 'Paysage héroïque'

De Piles specifically singles out Poussin as master of a type of noble or 'heroic' landscape in which the forms of nature are given a heightened grandeur, to accord with the noble theme generally depicted; the scene is also embellished with appropriately dignified architecture (corresponding to the 'tragic scene' of Vitruvius and his sixteenth-century commentator Serlio). As Verdi has observed, Poussin's reputation as a landscape artist in fact rests upon a relatively small number of works in which landscape plays a significant role.[26]

Although in other areas of his work Poussin was often contrasted with Titian (the master of 'le dessein' opposed to the practitioner of 'le coloris'), in the field of landscape Titian is cited as Poussin's most important predecessor, apart from the classical artist Apelles, painter of storm landscapes.[27] However, while Titian's landscapes are praised as supremely lifelike, those of Poussin are credited with improving upon nature, and combining truth to nature with nobility—in part by the addition of dignified architectural elements.[28]

As has been noted above, despite the official disdain of the category of landscape expressed by Félibien in his official role as *historiographe*, in the Preface to the *Conférences* of the Académie, nevertheless in the *Entretiens* themselves, and especially in the eighth Entretien, devoted to Poussin, Félibien shows himself responsive to its appeal, even though his chief interest is in the union of figures and landscape as expressing a particular theme or emotion. It is notable, for example, that writing of the *Moïse exposé* belonging to Jacques Stella, Félibien singles out the treatment of landscape before that of the subject: 'C'est un tableau

---

[25] Cf. *Cours*, p. 202.

[26] Cf. Verdi, op cit., p. 197. The paintings in question are the following: the *Seasons* (1660-1664), the *Phocion* pair (1648), *Diogenes* (c. 1648?), *Landscape with Polyphemus* (1650), *Orpheus and Eurydice* (c. 1649?), *Landscape with a Man Killed by a Snake* (1648), *Landscape with a Roman Road*, and *Landscape with Man Washing his Feet* (1648). All these, as Verdi notes, were engraved by the early eighteenth century in addition the *Orion* (1658?) never engraved, and *Pyramus and Thisbe* (1651?), not engraved until 1769, are of central importance (Verdi, loc. cit.).

[27] On Apelles see Pliny *Nat. Hist.*, XXXV, 96-7. Cf. also Félibien, *Ent.* V, p. 54, and Thuillier in 'Poussin et le paysage tragique : L'Orage Pointel au Musée des Beaux-Arts à Rouen', *La Revue du Louvre* (1976).

[28] An anon. writer (1678) claims that 'son architecture est d'une noblesse si charmante qu'il surpasse tous ceux qui s'en sont meslez jusques icy', *Le Songe d'Ariste*, cit. *Corpus*, p. 175.

admirable pour l'excellence du paysage, & de la sçavante maniere dont
le sujet est traité' (p. 64).

With Poussin's *Rebecca and Eliezar at the Well* of 1648 (Paris,
Louvre) it is above all 'l'union du paysage avec les figures' that is
praised, as creating an harmonious effect: 'un doux accord, & une
harmonie admirable, que se répand dans tout l'ouvrage' (p. 111).
Félibien goes on to praise Poussin's mastery in various aspects of the
work—colour, light and shade—which contribute to the overall effect
(pp. 150-51). In accordance with the requirements of decorum or
'convenance', Félibien stresses that no elements are out of character
with the prevailing mood of serenity: 'Le paisage n'a rien de solitaire',
recalling an idyllic golden age, 'la simplicité & la douceur de la vie des
premiers hommes [...]'. Among other elements, it is the treatment of
light which helps to create such a mood: the 'pur et serein' atmosphere
of the setting sun illuminates objects 'avec plus de douceur et de
tendresse [...]'.

Félibien praises the landscapes of the late 1640s precisely for the
variety of their 'dispositions', and also because they have as central
focus 'des sujets tirez de l'Histoire, ou de la Fable, ou de quelques
actions extraordinaires qui satisfont l'esprit & divertissent les yeux.' In
contrast to the *Rebecca and Eliezar*, where the mood is convivial, and
where 'il n'y a rien de solitaire', the *Landscape with Three Monks* (now
known to represent *Landscape with St Francis*—Belgrade, c. 1651) is a
'solitude', where 'l'on voit des Moines assis contre terre & appliquez à
la lecture.' (Pl. 1). A mood of contemplative reflection is evoked, for
Félibien, by this scene: 'un certain repos' equivalent to the 'tranquilleté'
experienced by the monks 'dans un désert si paisible & si charmant' (p.
60).

In contrast, the celebrated *Landscape with Man Killed by a Snake*
(London, National Gallery, 1648—Pl. 2) was seen by Félibien (and by
most succeeding critics) as inspiring 'l'horreur & la crainte' rather than
'repos'. Such an interpretation accords with the late seventeenth-century
emphasis on 'convenance' and on the expression of passions as the
dominant concerns of artistic theory. And later critics, including
notably Fénelon and Diderot, have (as has been shown) generally
followed this interpretation. In the imaginary dialogue between
Leonardo and Poussin, written by Fénelon and published posthumously
as one of the *Dialogues des morts*, the landscape is seen as a vehicle for
human emotions: 'un tableau bien triste', in Leonardo's supposed
words.[29] For Diderot also, writing in the *Salon* of 1767, the landscape is

---

[29] Fénelon, *Dialogue des morts*, *Œuvres* (1823 edition), pp. 340 ff.

Plate 1: Engraving after N. Poussin, *Landscape with three monks* ('Une solitude'). Photo: Witt Collection, Courtauld Institute of Art, negative no. 717 / 55(1).

Plate 2: Engraving by E. Baudet after N. Poussin, *Landscape with a man killed by a snake*. Photo: Witt Collection, Courtauld Institute of Art, negative no. B 64/572.

Plate 3: Engraving after N. Poussin, *Landscape with a storm.* British Museum, London, negative no. 251705.

Plate 4: Engraving by Vivares after N. Poussin, *Landscape with Pyramus and Thisbe*. Fitzwilliam Museum, Cambridge, accession no. 31.K.4-6; negative no. FMK.28475.

valued primarily as exhibiting a 'suite de passions différentes', and as having the idea of fear as its chief inspiration. For, in his view, it is only by the inclusion of some such human drama that a landscape is given the same validity as a history painting.[30]

In a general appreciation of Poussin's landscapes, towards the end of the eighth *Entretien*, Félibien praises the artist's 'intelligence' in depicting 'toutes sortes de paysages', and in rendering different species of tree, reflections in water, above all the subtle treatment of light and shade and aerial perspective—linking Poussin with Titian in his truth to nature here. (pp. 159-60) Félibien tacitly allows that it may on occasion be the moods of nature herself, rather than the 'mode' of a particular literary or historical theme, that dominates: he cites paintings in which 'il a représenté des tems calmes & sereins, dans d'autres, des pluyes, des vents & des orages, comme ceux que vous avez vus autrefois chez le sieur Pointel.' (The reference here is to the *Landscape with a Storm* (Rouen, Musée des Beaux-Arts—Pl. 3), painted for Pointel, and *Landscape with a Calm* (private coll.; both c.1651).[31] Félibien also quotes the artist's letter concerning *Pyramus and Thisbe* (Frankfurt, c. 1651—Pl. 4), in which he defines his aim as to render the effects of a storm, only incidentally, at the end of the letter, referring to the subject of the painting.[32] Félibien's emphasis in his conclusion is on the close association of subject and setting in Poussin's landscapes; he praises the artist's mastery of a wide range of subject-matter, and a storm scene such as *Pyramus and Thisbe*, depicting 'les effets les plus extraordinaires de la nature', is, in his view, validated, as it were, by the choice of a 'convenable' theme—'un sujet triste & lugubre' (pp. 60-61).

For de Piles, on the other hand, with his vision of the artist as emulating the divine Creator, the rendering of 'les effets [...] de la nature' was of prime importance, and landscape, as we have noted, occupies a higher place in his estimation. There is thus a different emphasis in his comments on Poussin's landscapes; in the *Conversations* of 1677, Léonidas, one of the two interlocutors, praises the 'compositions [...] nobles' and the 'fort belle' treatment of foliage, though the speaker then goes on to criticize the artist's treatment of light. De Piles's affiliations as 'coloriste' and champion of Rubens in the Académie are evident in the passage in the *Abrégé* of 1699, where he

---

[30] Diderot, 1767 *Salon*, in J. Seznec (ed.), *Le Salon de 1767* (Oxford, 1963), p. 268. Cf. also Verdi, op. cit., p. 202 ff.

[31] On these two landscapes see esp. Whitfield, 'Nicolas Poussin's *Orage* and *Tems calme*', *The Burlington Magazine*, 119 (1977), also Thuillier, 'Poussin et le paysage tragique'.

[32] For the letter, cf. Ch. Jouanny (ed.), *Correspondance de Nicolas Poussin* (Paris, 1911), p. 424, (no. 188 to Jacques Stella).

discusses Poussin's landscapes. He allows that these are 'admirables' on several counts, such as the choice of 'sites', and the variety of foliage, mentioning the subject of the landscape last: '[...] enfin par la singularité des sujets qu'il y fait entrer [...]' However, he again criticizes the treatment of light and shade, and also that of colour.[33]

Indeed, de Piles's criticism of Poussin's use of colour when applied to his figures is severe in the extreme: he claims that they are merely 'teintes générales', rather than 'l'imitation de celles du naturel qu'il ne voyoit que rarement [...]'. He allows that in landscape this deficiency is not so evident, though in his view this is simply because Poussin was forced to study nature rather than antique sculpture.[34]

III. 'Orientations nouvelles'

Let us now turn briefly to more recent critical opinion concerning two of Poussin's landscapes in particular: the *Landscape with a Storm*, and the National Gallery's *Landscape with a Man Killed by a Snake* of 1648. *L'Orage* is a pendant to the work described by Félibien as 'un tems calme et serein', which has recently been rediscovered.[35] One might in fact see a parallel here to Claude's habit of painting in pendants[36]; the pair may also embody a reflection of Poussin's 'theory of the modes', with their complementary themes and atmosphere.

For Thuillier, *L'Orage* represents an example of 'le paysage tragique', in which the artist shows '[...] la Nature saisie par une violence toute pareille à celle des personnes humaines' and is concerned to evoke 'les éléments déchaînés et semant la terreur ou la mort'.[37] He compares *L'Orage* with *Pyramus and Thisbe*, painted for Cassiano dal Pozzo c. 1651 (Frankfurt, Stadelsches Institut).[38] We have seen that Félibien quotes Poussin's own letter about this painting to Stella, according to which the mythological episode is present largely to provide a key to the meaning of the painting, where the human drama corresponds to the turbulence of nature. Bialostocki had also noted that Poussin here 'realizes' an idea drawn from Leonardo da Vinci, a

[33] De Piles, *Abrégé* (2nd. ed. 1715), pp. 457 ff. 'Réflexions sur les ouvrages de Poussin', p. 467.

[34] *Abrégé*, ed. cit., pp. 468-9 (cit. Thuillier, Corpus, p. 231).

[35] For a long time the *Orage* was known only through an engraving made before 1699, attributed to L. de Châtillon. Cf. G. Wildenstein, 'Les Gravures de Poussin au XVIIe siècle', GBA, 46 (1955), No. 189. See note 31 above.

[36] This was suggested by Whitfield, loc. cit.

[37] Thuillier, 'Poussin et le paysage tragique'.

[38] See Blunt, *Nicolas Poussin* (New Haven and London, 1966), vol. I p. 297; Verdi 'Poussin's Critical Fortunes', p. 198.

'recipe' for painting storms; Leonardo's *Trattato* was published in a French translation by Poussin's patrons (and with engravings based on Poussin's designs) in 1651.[39]

The *Orage* shows similar effects to those in Pyramus and Thisbe, as described by the artist himself, using the same motif of a bolt of lightning to indicate a tempest, although in the *Orage* the mythological incident is replaced by the foreground episode of travellers and animals. With its pendant the *Calme*, the subject appears, in Thuillier's view, to be the interlocking of human emotions with the violence or calm of nature.[40]

As Thuillier has reminded us, storm landscapes were not an innovation; indeed, 'tempêtes' were a speciality of Dughet.[41] But with Poussin the subject acquires a new seriousness, which, it is suggested, may derive from his study of human passions. When taken in the context of the series of landscapes painted in the years immediately preceding (1648-51), in which 'l'indifférence des élemens, la sérénité d'une Nature éternelle et féconde, s'opposent cruellement à l'échec du héros', the *Orage* and the *Calme*, by implicit analogy to human passions, may deserve to be classed as 'history paintings' rather than as landscapes.[42]

However, other recent analyses of Poussin's rendering of 'les tempêtes' have suggested that, rather than—or as well as—being concerned with the expression of human passions, it is closely linked to Neo-stoic conceptions of the 'storms of Fortune', and possibly more specifically to the disturbances of the Fronde in Paris. In a letter of June 1648 to Chantelou, concerning the series of *Sacraments* completed in that year, Poussin suggests that he planned to transform the *Sacraments* into another series of works depicting the 'tempests' of Fortune.[43] Several scholars, notably Verdi and McTighe, have recognized Charron's *De la sagesse* as the likely source.[44] Poussin's letter envisages a stratified world view, corresponding to three levels of natural abilities, from stupidity to wisdom, and propounds the Neo-stoic belief that man must attempt to stand firm when confronting the storms of Fortune.

---

[39] 'Une idée de Léonard réalisée par Poussin', *Revue des arts et des musées*, 4 (1954), pp. 134-5.

[40] Thuillier, op. cit.

[41] See N. Boisclair, *Gaspard Dughet, sa vie et son œuvre* (Paris, 1986), Cat. Nos. 134, 136, 801.

[42] Thuillier, loc. cit.

[43] *Correspondance*, p. 384.

[44] Verdi, 'Poussin and the Tricks of Fortune', *Burl. Mag.*, 124 (1982), and McTighe, 'Nicolas Poussin's Storm Landscapes and Libertinage in the mid-17th Century', *Word and Image*, 5, Nos. 3-4 (Oct-Dec 1989) pp. 359-60.

In her exploration of the intellectual context of this passage, McTighe
has identified parallels with Charron's writings, in particular the
concept of three layers of air within the earth's atmosphere which are
seen as aligned with three levels of mankind in the social order.[45]
Charron distinguishes the three parts that make up man as body, mind
and soul; the soul, the 'middle level', parallels the middle level of the
atmosphere—the area containing 'météores' (in the seventeenth century
a synonym for 'tempest'). According to the *libertins*, the deity was
replaced by the concept of Fortune, who was equated with laws
governing the cycles of death and regeneration, storm and calm.
Indeed, it is likely that, in view of Poussin's close relations with *libertin*
circles in both Paris and Rome, their ideas may have prompted his
interest in Charron's text.[46] Verdi has suggested that several of
Poussin's late landscapes may represent a fulfilment of his aim to
represent the 'tours de fortune' as moral exemplars.[47] However, these
landscapes do not form a series in the true sense, as they were
commissioned by different patrons, and are of varying sizes and
formats.[48] It seems probable that the group of landscapes depicting
storms springs from the comment about 'tempests of Fortune'—the
Orage and *Calme* may be linked with *Polyphemus* and *Hercules and
Cacus*, as an allegorical representation of the cycle of tempest to clear
weather, and also with Orion, an allegory of the workings of a
thunderstorm.[49] In the light of these allegorical depictions of storms,
Poussin's main idea appears to be to present an image not solely of
human passion but also of man's subsequent blindness.[50]

Another work which has formed the focus of much discussion and re-
interpretation is the *Landscape with a Man Killed by a Snake* (London,
National Gallery), painted for Pointel in 1648. It should be seen in
relation to the *Landscape with a Man Pursued by a Snake* (Montreal,
Museum of Fine Arts).[51] The Montreal landscape has been seen as 'an
early experiment in the dispersal of fear through a landscape', which

---

[45] Charron, *Œuvres* (1635, facs. ed., 1970), vol. 2, pp. 154-5; McTighe, loc. cit.

[46] McTighe, loc. cit.

[47] Verdi proposes the Phocion landscapes, *Man Killed by a Snake*, the death of Eurydice in
Orpheus and Eurydice, the suicides in *Pyramus and Thisbe*, 'Poussin and the Tricks of Fortune'.

[48] This was pointed out by McTighe, loc. cit.

[49] McTighe, loc. cit. The subject of the *Orion* was recognized by Gombrich in 'The Subject of
Poussin's *Orion*', *Burl. Mag.*, 84 (1944), reprinted in *Symbolic Images* (London, 1972).

[50] McTighe cites the response of the human figures in both the *Orage* and *Pyramus*, the effect of
the tempest being literally blinding.

[51] Commissioned by Pozzo in the early 1640s; formerly in Blunt coll. Cf. entry by McTighe in
Claude to Corot, p. 56.

reached its fullest formulation in the National Gallery landscape of 1648.[52] And there are of course numerous classical allusions to the idea of the treacherous snake lurking in the grass — again echoing the Stoic belief in the need to guard against unpredictable fate, and also alluding to the presence of mortality in an idyllic natural setting.[53]

The National Gallery landscape of 1648 was, as we have seen, interpreted by Félibien as expressing 'the effects of fear'.[54] The aim of depicting the 'passions of the soul' was central to seventeenth-century artistic theory and practice. Félibien himself did not identify the figures with any classical source, yet the scene presented appears so specific that some writers have attempted to identify textual sources, and have suggested that it may represent an actual historical event.[55] However, a more widely held view is that the artist's concern is rather to present a general concept relating to the presence of death within nature.[56]

Recent scholarship has demonstrated that in fact Poussin's own intentions would in all probability have more in common with a less logical, more arcane and 'hieroglyphic' approach, found in the Barberini circle in Rome in which the artist moved. In her recent illuminating discussion of the painting, McTighe has suggested that the key to understanding both snake landscapes may in fact be found in mid-seventeenth-century interpretation of antiquities, and in particular the contemporary study of hieroglyphs as a form of allegory.[57] As she has demonstrated, Kircher, in the late 1630s, began the first modern attempt to translate the Egyptian hieroglyphs visible in Rome. His procedure was to collate the meanings given to hieroglyphs within spurious Renaissance literature on Egyptian writings.[58] There are numerous hieroglyphs of the serpent; for Kircher, the snake was always connected with the idea of death putrescence and rebirth, and he also inferred from late antique texts that the coiling body of the snake was an image of the twisting path of the sun travelling through the zodiac. Thus the snake that inspires terror in Poussin's protagonists may have borne a particular range of associations for Poussin's circle; both as a pictograph of mortality and as a reminder of regeneration implied in

---

[52] Cf. Verdi in exhibition catalogue, *Poussin and Cézanne* (Edinburgh), pp. 67-8.

[53] Op. cit. p. 69.

[54] It is significant that E. Baudet's engraving after the painting carries an inscription to this effect.

[55] Cf. for instance Blunt, *Nicolas Poussin*, vol. I, pp. 286-7.

[56] Verdi, *Poussin and Cézanne*, p. 69.

[57] McTighe, 'The Hieroglyphic Landscape and the Late Allegories of Nicolas Poussin', unpublished thesis (Yale Univ., 1987); cf. also her entry on Montreal, *Man Pursued by Snake*, in *Claude to Corot*, pp. 50-56.

[58] A full bibliography of Kircher's writings is given in McTighe.

the cycle of the seasons. Such 'hieroglyphic' meanings reinforce the generally felt interpretation of the 'snake' landscapes as representing human mortality. For McTighe, these landscapes do portray the 'effects of fear', but go beyond that in embodying an allegory of nature's processes expressed in hieroglyphic form.[59] In such interpretations, then, we have a reversion to a pre-classical (indeed, pre-scientific) view of nature, whereby human fate is seen both as integral with the processes of nature, and as emblematic; we are indeed presented with a 'paysage moralisé', but with a very different moral emphasis from that implied by later seventeenth-century and eighteenth-century intepretations. The 'orientations anciennes'—as represented by the late seventeenth-century writings of Félibien and de Piles—interpret the artist's landscapes very much in terms of the current preoccupations with the 'noble' subject and with the play of human passions (the latter concern in particular dominated too in the writings of Fénelon and Diderot). More recent 'readings'—'orientations nouvelles'—have in some cases tended to stress, rather, the interlocking correspondence of man and nature—even the predominance of nature over man (as well as pointing to possible possible social or historical connotations). And in the 'newest' of such readings, we find the unexpected connection (especially regarding the 'snake' landscapes and the late mythological landscapes) with the more arcane and mysterious world of the hieroglyph—a very different world from that illuminated by the light of Cartesian rationalism. While many of Poussin's landscapes may indeed be 'heroic', in de Piles's term, incorporating noble subjects and dignified architecture, their roots may none the less perhaps be found in a more primitive world-view, according to which the very processes of nature form the central theme.

---

[59] McTighe stresses the relevance of Poussin's contact with the *libertins*, especially their belief in Nature as a model for human nature.

Descartes and Pascal:
metaphorical sabotage by stealth

BY

ELIZABETH MOLES

UNIVERSITY OF GLASGOW

Descartes and Pascal metaphorically decapitate the authoritarian 'I' of conventional discourse as they weave complex counter-responsions to traditional Western philosophy and religious apologetic. In the *Méditations* and the *Pensées* they challenge, respectively, the stale learning by rote imposed by scholasticism upon its acolytes, and the dusty abstractions of traditional Christian apologetic argument. With refreshing brio, each author carves out new paths for his persona, engaging the interlocutor directly in an aggressive dialogue on moral and epistemological principles. Although Cartesian metaphor normally operates in schists, preferring the solid signifiers of architecture, rock and clay, its fundamental structure is anarchist. Witness the revolutionary zeal with which Descartes winches out Porphyrys's tree to replant it upon the airy roots of metaphysics: 'toute la Philosophie est comme un arbre, dont les racines sont la métaphysique, le tronc est la physique, et les branches qui sortent de ce tronc sont toutes les autres sciences, qui se réduisent à trois principales, à savoir la médecine, la mécanique et la morale'[1] (III, 779-800). Rightly did Pierre Mesnard stress the vitality of this image: it constitutes a deliberate inversion of the traditional neo-platonist tree, which was devised to tease out the separate strands of knowledge.[2] For the purpose of this article we are bypassing rhetorical device as clichéd sop to the hypothetical *honnête*

---

[1] Page references in the text are from Descartes, *Œuvres*, ed. F. Alquié, 3 vol. (Paris, 1963-73), henceforward abbreviated to F. A. Alquié gives references to the Adam-Tannery edition (Paris, 1897-1913), in the margins of the Garnier edition.

[2] P. Mesnard, 'L'Arbre de la sagesse', *Cahiers de Royaumont, Philosophie*, II, *Descartes* (New York, 1957), pp. 336-59, notably pp. 341-4. See also G. Rodis-Lewis, 'Limites du modèle mécanique dans la "disposition" des organes', *L'Anthropologie cartésienne* (Paris, 1990), pp. 161-7.

homme , in order to focus upon the fundamental tropes generating new imaginative discourse, which structure and quicken an author's cast of thought in the ways defined by Spoerri's brilliant paper on Cartesian writing, and the subsequent discussion which distinguishes between dead and revitalising metaphor.[3]

Overthrowing Suarez's scholasticism, Descartes devises a finely-honed pure logic in order to elaborate his own philosophy, integrating different fields of knowledge into the ambit of his universal method.[4] Pascal's thought is impregnated with this logic, as it is with the paradigms of infinite greatness and smallness evoked in the *Principes*, which was probably his first introduction to philosophy.[5] Revolting with fulgurating ferocity against a metaphysical view of man, Pascal creates metaphorical structures which critically question the validity of the existential struggle enacted by the *Méditations*. Although he ventriloquizes its noological purity of utterance in the *Pensées* in order to express the epistemic plight of Everyman, his 'I' attains neither philosophic freedom nor transcendence. These writers enact a deliberate sabotage of their weighty intellectual precursors, whereby metaphor, 'bolt true' to their deepest preoccupations is no mere fashionable foil, but carries ontological weight. We experience the force of Lichtenberg's maxim: 'La métaphore est toujours plus intelligente que son auteur', subtly emended by Alquié to 'autrement intelligente que son auteur'.[6] Weary metaphors of the past are infused with coruscating new energy.

Contrast the messianic vision of Descartes as charted in the *Olympiques* (10.11.1619) with that of Pascal's *Mémorial* (23.11.1654) thirty-five years later.[7] Descartes emerges from his dream reassured that: 'l'Esprit de Vérité [...] avait voulu lui ouvrir les trésors de toutes les sciences par ce songe'.[8] The contrast reveals a Pascal encased in Cartesian armature at his moment of destiny. In his night of fire he

---

[3] T. Spoerri, 'La Puissance métaphorique de Descartes', *Cahiers*, pp. 273-87, and pp. 295-9 of the discussion.

[4] Most of the scholastic references are in E. Gilson, *Index Scholastico-Cartésien* (Paris, 1913). Descartes's stand on the eternal truths is argued against Suarez, *Disputationes Metaphysicae*, XXXII.

[5] On this see M. Le Guern, *Pascal et Descartes* (Paris, 1971), pp. 41-50 and p. 125: 'Tout porte à penser que la lecture des *Principes* a été pour Pascal non seulement une initiation à la philosophie cartésienne, mais même une initiation à la philosophie tout court.'

[6] See Spoerri, art. cit., p. 273, and Alquié's intervention p. 299.

[7] The Latin text is in AT, X, 217-219, this translation in F. A. I, pp. 52-63. References to the *Pensées* are from the *Œuvres complètes*, ed. L. Lafuma (Paris, 1963). The *Mémorial* is fr. 913.

[8] F. A. I, p. 57. On p. 59 the Spirit of Truth is compared to 'La foudre [...] qui descendit sur lui pour le posséder'. For the philosopher truth and mythical metaphor fuse in this vision.

bows before the salvific 'Dieu d'Abraham, Dieu d'Isaac, Dieu de Jacob'. This positive incandescent vision is instantly counterchecked by negative backfire directed against Descartes in the following line of the manuscript: 'Dieu [...] non des philosophes et des savants'. The oscillation is prolonged in the seraphic: 'Certitude, certitude, sentiment, joie, paix.' 'Certitude' inscribes religious ecstasy as against rational cogency. Provocatively Pascal ascribes certainty to 'sentiment' as opposed to reason. The fundamental inscription is that of Derridean 'différance'. By adopting his insights we may fruitfully show how Pascal constructs certain key metaphors that underpin his metaphysics upon a system of 'différance' to Descartes, mindful of the fact that in Derrida, 'différances' do not necessarily entail positive advances in philosophy.[9] Rather, they represent a different position within long-established patterns of thinking, differences, which, by deconstructing the opposition, violently reverse or question a previous hierarchy. The creation of such 'différance' is a prerequisite for the advance of philosophical thought. Cartesian Logos is crucified by the 'Dieu de Jésus-Christ'. It is quintessentially Pascalian to structure his thought in dialectical blocks of positives versus negatives.

Contrast fr.427, regarded by Port-Royal as the introduction to the apologetic, which, to paraphrase Johnson's definition of metaphor, offers another violent yoking-together of heterogeneities:

> Je ne sais qui m'a mis au monde, ni ce que c'est que le monde, ni que moi-même [...] je ne sais ce que c'est que mon corps [...] cette partie même de moi qui pense ce que je dis, qui fait réflexion sur tout et sur elle-même et ne se connaît non plus que tout le reste. Je vois ces effroyables espaces de l'univers [...] et je me trouve attaché à un coin de cette vaste étendue, sans que je sache pourquoi . Tout ce que je connais est que je dois bientôt mourir.

Although the bludgeoning 'qui' and 'que', the relentless probing of knowledge and ignorance is Cartesian, the suspension of the 'moi' in a Miltonian dark and limitless bound of infinity, and an eternity of remorseless time induces a non-Cartesian plangency. Time in Descartes belongs to the present enouncer; it is always subservient to his thought processes. His grip on it is assured. In Pascal every aspiration, every razor-sharp question of an 'I', who mouths negatives with Beckettian futility, is sucked into the agonised inevitability of implacable death. Could these lines, orchestrating man's everlasting questions about identity and purpose with such pointed lyricism, have been penned before Descartes pared man to an icicle of consciousness in an epistemic

[9] D. Wood expounds this most lucidly: 'Difference and the problems of strategy', in D. Wood and R. Bernasconi (eds), *Derrida and Différance* (Warwick, 1983), pp. 93-106.

void? I submit that they could not. The technique of 'renversement continuel du pour au contre' (fr. 93) operates with surgical precision against Cartesian confidence. In the second *Méditation* we scaled a vertiginous pyramid of ontological interrogations: 'ne me suis-je donc pas aussi persuadé que je n'étais point? Non certes, j'étais sans doute, si je me suis persuadé, ou seulement si j'ai pensé quelque chose'. (II, 415) Our triumphant philosopher promptly quashes his imaginary antagonist: 'Il n'y a donc point de doute que je suis, s'il me trompe; et qu'il me trompe tant qu'il voudra, il ne saurait jamais faire que je ne sois rien, tant que je penserai être quelque chose.' There follows the splendid ringing conviction: 'il faut conclure que cette proposition: *je suis, j'existe* est nécessairement vraie'. Both authors juggle exquisitely positive affirmation against negative soul-searching. Pascal's monologue splayed the objectivity of 'savoir' into negatives prior to converting it into the traumatic personal 'connaître' of dusky death. Yet to dash the brave new Cartesian world by nightmarish metaphor of time and space scarcely constitutes a routing of Cartesian logic which can and does resist such assault. Both authors suspend the 'I' in a time-warp, freezing consciousness in order that they may strip from it any mundane perception of consubtantiality. Is, however, Pascal's rhetoric against reason mere rodomontade, fuelled by the Jansenist metaphorical and existential view of man? The answer is far from simple.

On the purely expository level the network of Cartesian metaphor offers the perfect mimesis of orderly progression towards truth, forging a concatenation of new insights into physics, geometry, and metaphysics, teaching us through the 'longues chaînes de raisons dont les géomètres ont coutume de se servir' (I, 587), how to bind all knowledge together. At the other extreme, Pascal's 'image de la condition humaine' as 'un nombre d'hommes dans les chaînes et tous condamnés à la mort, dont les uns étant chaque jour égorgés à la vue des autres' (fr. 434), might serve as subject for a scarifying canvas by Bacon. Repeatedly does the shibboleth of death impose traumatic arrest of consciousness. Here the bloody butchery of hapless men in chains dialectically transforms the steel links of Cartesian structures in a clear case of emotional transference. This image, monodic in Descartes, operates like a gamma ray in the *Écrits sur la grâce* illuminating the ambivalence of man's free will since the fall of Adam. In order to render the 'considération métaphysique' of the dual nature of human liberty comprehensible, Pascal puts chains into the hands of Everyman's two friends. They personify, respectively, grace versus the hypnotic delectation of concupiscence: 'enfin figurons-nous que ces deux amis le tirent avec chacun sa chaîne, mais avec différente force, n'est-il pas visible qu'il suivra le plus fort?'[10] (705) The ambivalent comedy points the commonsense moral: 'qu'y a-t-il de plus clair que cette proposition, que l'on fait toujours ce qui délecte le plus?' (704), underpinning Pascal's Jansenist polemic in favour of the Augustinian tenet: '*Quod amplius delectat, secundam id operemur necesse est*' (704).[11] In its diabolic yet absurdist hyberbole this tug of war dramatises the haplessness that is man's lot. A stark antithesis to Descartes's empowering sequential chains of reason!

The artist Pascal superimposes a further level of exegesis by meditating on the inadequacy of the chain metaphor to express the tragic emotional dilemma of fallen man: 'Cette comparaison explique à peu près son état, mais non pas parfaitement, parce qu'il est impossible de trouver dans la nature aucune comparison qui convienne parfaitement aux actions de la volonté' (705-6). With uncanny prescience he encapsulates the insights of modern linguistic philosophy by pointing to the hiatus between sign and signified. Whereas Descartes, more sensitive to the 'pièges' of philosophical than of ordinary language, manipulated the image with scissor-like precision, Pascal unravels its ambiguity, expressing the unbridgeable gulf between stylistic resource and the abrasive reality of our experience of conflict. When Pascal acknowledges, with a diffident irony, the intricate constraints of metaphorical exegesis, we recall the value he laid on concrete representation in apologetic. This attains maximum force in his wicked jibe at the abstruse Cartesian proofs of God: 'Quand un homme serait persuadé que les proportions des nombres sont des vérités immatérielles, dépendantes d'une première vérité en qui elles subsistent, et qu'on appelle Dieu, je ne le trouverai pas beaucoup avancé pour son salut.' (fr. 449) Pascal was initially requested to engage in Jesuit-Jansenist controversy over grace because of his ability to couch issues in terms appealing to the *honnête homme,* and we all know that the popularity of the *Provinciales* was spectacular. Yet it is fascinating to find that the agonised eighteenth letter reiterates the paradoxical tensions between chains and the *divertissement* that will become a fundamental category in the *Pensées* as Pascal returns to that seminal Augustinian quotation '*Quod amplius* [...]' in a final frenetic endeavour to clear Port-Royal of heresy by adducing 'des vérités de fait' and

---

[10] Page references are to Mesnard's magisterial re-editing of this text in *Œuvres complètes, Œuvres diverses, 1654-1657,* III (Paris 1991).

[11] The source in Augustine is *Opera* IV (Paris, 1614), p. 390, and as Mesnard points out in note 2, it is also quoted in Jansenius, *Augustinus,* III, L. IV, Ch. 6, Louvain, 1641, col. 412, and in *Provinciale* XVIII.

buttressing them with textual quotations.[12] When we read the opening *Provinciales* we respond to the delicious punning on 'prochain' as adjective and noun, and on the insufficiency of a grace that is ostensibly 'suffisant', punning designed by Pascal to appeal to the 'bonne foi' of the average citizen. Compare them to the equally deceptive simplicity of Part I of the *Discours*: which salutes 'le bon sens' before Descartes proceeds from good sense to certain truth as evinced in geometric rules, and to an elaborate metaphysical demonstration of God's existence. May we not infer a rivalry that is simultaneously aesthetic and philosophical? Is Pascal mimicking the Cartesian project by framing the propositions of grace in the vulgar accessible context of 'le sens commun'?[13]

In his magisterial new edition of the *Écrits* Mesnard deconstructs the idiosyncratic geometric reasoning whereby Pascal circumscribes the feebleness of Pelagian objections to the basic tenets of Trent.[14] Parish underlines the fascinating ambiguity with which Pascal points the impossibility of settling the debate on grace.[15] However Mesnard highlights the subtlety with which Pascal isolates certain common-sense principles at the heart of the quarrel as he sets out the propositions of grace in geometric order.[16] By refusing to 'enchaîner les propositions en allant des principes aux conséquences' Pascal opts to substitute 'des propositions équivalentes', with the result that, rather than establishing new doctrine, he refines the old by refracting it in a new light.[17] Pascal most cunningly frames the more rebarbative propositions of grace according to a Cartesian perspective. His debunking appeal to common sense presupposes an improbable consensus on the intricated Catholic doctrine of faith and salvation. He then endeavours to confound counter-polemic with geometric reasoning braced by metaphor. When discussing the seminal chain metaphor, Mesnard argues that the piquant absurdity of this 'supposition métaphysique' explodes the Molinist premise that each man has sufficient grace to resist concupiscence.[18] Pascal's subsequent development on grace supports Mesnard's thesis: 'La

---

[12] Cognet in his edition of *Les Provinciales* (Paris, 1965), pp. XXVII, XXVIII and XXX describes how Pascal was invited to join the debate in order to leaven Arnauld's ponderousness, and how the public welcomed every letter as a 'divertissement'.

[13] See for a complex unravelling of the term the recent article by J-M. Beyssade, 'La transformation du sens commun', *Revue de métaphysique et de morale* (no. 4, 1991), pp. 497-514.

[14] See his edition, pp. 626-36.

[15] R. Parish, *Pascal's Lettres Provinciales: A Study in Polemic* (Oxford, 1989), pp. 135-45, 176-88.

[16] See especially p. 623.

[17] Mesnard, p. 625.

[18] Ibid., p. 629.

méthode géométrique, même employée d'une façon négative, comporte un envers positif [...] elle appuie la vérité en la rendant plausible' by showing how: 'l'erreur se redouble et prend deux formes contraires'.[19] It is only when analysed from our Cartesian perspective that Pascal's transmogrification of certain dogmas is less disconcerting. The caricaturing of entrenched theological positions replicates his conscious caricature of geometric reasoning and metaphor in the *Pensées.*

Nonetheless, the 'renversement du pour au contre' does not offer a slick paradigm which might unlock the *différance* between Descartes and Pascal. The dialectic it represents is too crude for the intricate inscription of thought and word pattern. Its simplicity expresses itself in the sharp horizontal layering between Pascal's three orders of reality and truth adumbrated in *Provinciale* XVIII, fully separated in fr. 308, which ranks materialists, intellectuals and spiritual leaders in ascending order, distinguishing truth as apprehended by the senses and the spirit. It cannot subsume the vertical radiation from the ultimate spiritual order of charity that expresses the divine plan, which, as Pierre Magnard has shown brilliantly, dictates mobile spiral progressions between orders that operate in chiaroscuro.[20] Pascal reshapes the monolithic 'ordre des raisons', rewriting his sources : 'As what and when, and how and where I choose' with a feverish appropriation that transcends mere contradiction. Descartes specifies his own structures of metaphor and method, his own mechanistic view of the world. Pascal specifies an ultimate 'ordre de la charité' where Christians are 'membres pensants' of the vine representing the church (frs. 360, 372). His predilection for the Cartesian adjective 'pensant' should not disguise a radical dislocation. The coiled tensions of the image of man as 'roseau pensant' (fr. 200) convey an expressionistic, Munch-like consciousness of the human tragedy that is alien to our solipsistic philosopher, to whom the 'soumission de la raison' enjoined by Jansenist doctrine would have been anathema. Nonetheless the Christian-Cartesian disjunction of discourse is built into Pascal's most controversial meditations, forcing the interlocutor in the dialogue of the *Pensées* to examine Cartesian parameters of enquiry. Let us trace the broad outlines of its structure.

If we interrogate our writers as to their starting point in the material world, the basic concept of the 'point' elicits forked replies. In *Méditation* 2, Descartes's 'lumière naturelle' provides the insight necessary to fulfil his yearning for the Archimedean 'point fixe et assuré' in space and time whence he may strike out in his bold quest for

---

19 Ibid., p. 631.

20 P. Magnard, *Nature et histoire dans l'apologétique de Pascal* (Paris, 1975), notably pp. 77-90.

mastery of nature. Contrast the 'point indivisible' Pascal so frequently
invoked as a source of inexhaustible mystery for the rational mind. As
soon as man seeks to graft spatial and metaphoric correlatives onto the
mathematical point, he is whirled aloft into vertiginous perplexities. As
Marin shows, Pascal's indivisible, shrinking and vanishing point, that
quintessence of geometry and matter is 'un néant d'espace', when fixed
it is a 'néant de mouvement' so that men occupy a fibrillating fulcrum in
the middle, where the 'point fixe et assuré' forever eludes them.[21]

In the fourth *Méditation* Descartes traces the geography of our being
with precise delicacy. Man, a 'milieu entre Dieu et le néant' occupies a
median state between sovereign being and non-being (II, 457). His
participation in Being generates the felicitous state of assurance that he
will not be led into error; conversely, his participation in non-being
exposes him to: 'une infinité de manquements de façon que je ne me dois
pas étonner si je me trompe'. In fr. 199 Pascal's man, 'un milieu entre
rien et tout' derives zero security from his spatial anchoring. Indeed the
Cartesian artery linking knowledge to existence is severed. Their
error-prone subject straddles the irreconcilable dichotomy of being
'incapable de savoir certainement et d'ignorer absolument', but
Pascalian man lacks any method of clearly distinguishing certain truths.
Whereas Cartesian man may: 'sans témérité rechercher les fins
impénétrables de Dieu', Pascalian man is cautioned against just such
'témérité', that favourite seventeenth-century term for religious
hubris.[22] Philosophers who aim to 'parler de tout', (although Descartes
is implicated here Pascal cannily does not name him), incur a contumely
which is the more ironic because Descartes's work so stimulated his
development. So the physical plight of man, caught beween the receding
infinities of greatness and smallness, whose mysteries were magnified
infinitely by telescope and microscope in that century, is compounded
by his failure to understand the principles governing the space into
which he is unceremoniously thrust. Hence the melodious, haunting
melancholy of the alexandrine: 'Le silence éternel de ces espaces infinis'
fizzles out not with a bang but a whimper into the diminutive personal
pronoun 'm'effraie' (fr. 201). In contrast the third *Méditation* ends
where fr. 199 began, in rapt not fearful contemplation of God and his
works for here Descartes marvels at 'l'incomparable beauté de cette
immense lumière' (II, 454). Pascal consciously uses space and time as a
source of metaphor rather than an object of scientific study. *Qua* poet

[21] L. Marin, *La Critique du discours* (Paris, 1975), pp. 404-408.

[22] F. A., II, p. 458. Jesuitical temerity is condemned in the *Provinciales*, ed. cit., pp. 44, 213,
277, 317, 328, 343, 345; temerity in general in fr. 60, 199 and 427 of the *Pensées*.

he shreds them, using Cartesian terms of investigation not in order to establish progressive parameters within which we can experiment and achieve mastery of nature, but rather to convince blasted reason of its privation. Brushing aside Descartes's exorcism of the demon doubt, he strikes dread of mortality into the soul.

Let us therefore compare their treatment of Pyrrhonism. We have perhaps overstated Descartes's self-assurance. He was sufficiently racked by doubt to create a brilliant and enduring metaphysical metaphor in the imaginative fiction of the 'mauvais génie, non moins rusé et trompeur que puissant'.[23] The dramatic force of this Mephistophelian genie captivated Pascal, polemicist extraordinary, who, as we have seen, has elective affinities with Goethe's 'Geist der stets verneint'.[24] As epistemic artifice it enables Descartes to conduct a ferocious duel of wits: 'Je suppose donc que toutes les choses que je vois sont fausses, je pense n'avoir aucun sens: je crois que le corps, la figure, l'étendue, et le mouvement et le lieu ne sont que des fictions de mon esprit' (415). With a supreme assertion of will, Descartes hypothesises that his positive apprehensions of himself and of the physical world should be construed into negatives only to transcend this hyperbolical doubt by affirming the primordial intellectual consciousness that informs the thinking self. In Descartes inference presupposes performance, thought empowers. The reverse is true for Pascal, who grounds our metaphysical identity in the desolate myth of the Fall of man. The thought on which Descartes predicates his existence gains in richness as the *res cogitans* becomes: 'une chose qui doute, qui conçoit, qui affirme, qui nie, qui veut, qui ne veut pas et qui sent' (420-1). Descartes channels us further into the tunnel of his implacable search for infallible truth, yoking gritty insights with rivets of 'qui' and 'que'. His metaphysical fiction deconstructs and reconstructs an original 'I' for whom thought constitutes a purely cerebral structure of reason, passion, and sentience, negative and positive modes of consciousness. For Pascal's fictive unbeliever intellectual argument is larded with an earthy practicality that confounds logical analysis. Investigating Pyrrhonism in fr. 131, he conducts a farcical dialogue, daring the benighted sceptic to doubt 'si on le pince'. This *reductio ad absurdum*: yields to the stentorian injunction 'Humiliez-vous raison impuissante' calculated to give the lie direct to Descartes.

---

[23] F.A., II, *Méd.* I, p. 412; the term 'malin génie' comes from the Latin text *genium malignum*, p. 181.

[24] Goethe, *Faust, Erster Teil, Studierzimmer*, Hamburger Ausgabe (München,1986), p. 47.

Yet almost immediately the tensions of attraction and repulsion to
Descartes fuse as the apologist-scientist concedes to the enemy in the
immortal lines: 'Certes il n'y a rien qui choque plus notre raison que de
dire que le péché du premier homme ait rendu coupables ceux qui étant
si éloignés de cette source semblent incapables d'y participer. Il nous
semble même très injuste' thereby scandalising his friends at Port-
Royal. Are we not, therefore, at liberty to traduce Pascal's gibe at the
Cartesian 'roman de la matière' by designating the metaphor of sin as
the 'roman du péché' and inferring by analogy that in each case dogma
impedes appropriate rational investigation?

The elevation as opposed to the humiliation of thought leads us to a
complex sabotage of Cartesianism in the Pascalian wager, whose
original title was 'Infini: rien'. He begins by positing the infinite
incomprehensibility of God in whose presence Man is 'rien'. Conversely
Descartes deduced from the idea of infinity, unique in its harmonious
plenitude, a basis for proving the objective existence of the eternal
truths. His God of ontological metaphor stands at the antipodes of the
brooding Jansenist deity, Pascal presented Him as insulated inhabitant of
a glossy bubble of abstract truth, floating above moral preoccupation,
unconcerned with man's salvation. For Descartes God represented the
only salvation that mattered, that of truth. His sterile deity offers a
radiant and compelling formal purity of abstraction.

In order to create an alternative temptation , Pascal seduces us with
the God offering the aphrodisiac of vicarious gain. After stranding
reason on a traffic island by the triple (is the trinity of negation
deliberate?) assertion that it cannot prove God's existence, Pascal
imperiously beckons it to his aid as he number-crunches into snippets
the infinite chances of profit and loss that his interlocutor might incur,
were he to take out shares in an eternity of bliss, by accepting his
enticing wager. With mathematical rigour Pascal bludgeons his
opponent into accepting that it is reasonable to make the wager to live as
if God exists. Reason cannot prove the more desirable part of the
equation: namely that God exists. If the distinction is Cartesian, the
gravamen of the argument is not, though, to Pascal's undying credit and
Port-Royal's undying ire, the distinction is not fudged. To make his case
Pascal employs the metaphorical 'règle des partis' as opposed to the
austere 'règles de la méthode.' We forsake the brutal 'renversement du
pour au contre' as we are jerked by mathematical deduction through the
branches of the Cartesian tree into the wager which elaborates the idea
of infinite chances to compound our gains if we live as though God
exists. Mesmerised by the logic of the Absurd as he operates his brilliant
patented rule, Pascal guides us through hooplike sequences of finite

versus infinite *hasards* which conspire to compute that we should bet one out of two or three lives to gain one out of two, let alone an infinite number of lives, even if the chances were infinitely weighted against us: 'Cela est démonstratif et si les hommes sont capables de quelque vérité, celle-là l'est' (fr. 418) cries Pascal with Cartesian fervour. Philosophical checkmate.

Transformation of structures proceeds apace. After the fiendishly detailed computation, (certain French mathematicians stress that Pascal's deductions rival those of Descartes in their minuteness), the apologist reinserts the Cartesian metaphor of the body-machine to suggest a less stressful use of our intellect: amputate your reason, suspend disbelief, embrace Catholic dogma, go to Mass, take holy water.[25] With simian dexterity he bids the decapitated 'I' swing from Cartesian branches. The *chiquenaude*: 'il faut parier. Cela n'est pas volontaire, vous êtes embarqués' leads us with stupendous audacity into the second nudge: 'vous voulez aller à la foi et vous n'en savez pas le chemin.' It is every whit as breathtaking as the *chiquenaude* with which Pascal allegedly accused Descartes of launching his God into motion: *Je ne puis pardonner à Descartes: il voudrait bien se pouvoir passer de Dieu; mais il n'a pu s'empêcher de lui donner une chiquenaude pour mettre le monde en mouvement; après cela, il n'a plus que faire de Dieu* (fr. 1001). We may make bold to object against our apologist: 'après quoi il n'aura plus que faire de la raison raisonnante'.[26] Descartes's 'chemin' imposed its own rigour; in Pascal, coercion has replaced reasoning. The gloss on the square-bashing advice: 'cela vous fera croire et vous abêtira.' is designed to browbeat the rational seventeenth-century *honnête homme* into subservience. Again a key metaphor illustrating 'différance.'

By substituting the cardinal rules of betting for those of reasoning, Pascal violently wrenches the Cartesian automaton into a radically foreign structuralist mode. The brainwashed interlocutor, confronted with the hoops of set routines, supplicates comically—or is it tragically?—'j'ai les mains liées et la bouche muette [...] on me force à parier et je ne suis pas en liberté, on ne me relâche pas'. Compare the graphic sketches of the three opening *Méditations* which precede the initial twists in the argument. Descartes, reposing beside the fire in his

---

[25] See the comment by M. Beth, *Cahiers de Royaumont*, pp. 292-3.

[26] Le Guern correctly points out that this is the specific position taken by Hyperaspistes, who contradicts Descartes, op cit., pp. 168-9. The reference is to F. A. II, Lettre à ***, août 1641 (pp. 368-74), which argues the uniqueness of the divine Being. I submit that the tenor of the criticism encapsulates Pascal's general impatience with metaphysical proofs of God's existence, hence he would have applied the 'chiquenaude' metaphor equally to Descartes in a polemical context.

dressing-gown in the first, is suspended in agitated trance between sleeping and dreaming. In the second, he is bemused enough to wonder if he has fallen into a pool of deep water, and enumerates the parts of his body prior to describing in minute detail the extraction of his famous piece of wax from the hive before it is melted in the fire.[27] Compare, above all, Descartes's clenched effort to slough off bodily preoccupation at the very opening of the third Méditation on God's existence: 'Je fermerai maintenant les yeux, je boucherai mes oreilles, j'effacerai même de ma pensée toutes les images des choses corporelles'. Liberated Cartesian man follows the imperative of reason, engaging the whole self in the pursuit of clear and distinct perception of the alterity of God, the nature of matter, and the soul-body divide. Only at the end of the third meditation does the philosopher adopt the posture Pascalian man strikes at the opening of fr. 199, and allow his 'esprit ébloui' leisure to marvel at the beauty of God's creation (II, 454). Descartes's vocabulary here will be echoed in 'Disproportion'. The exercise of his reason precedes, but does not supersede, contemplation of light. The Pascalian *pari*, a fundamental metaphor for faith, rationalises the irrationality of the fanatical conviction that belief may be enforced by a dull and brutish routine inflecting the will towards God. Is it then a simulacrum of Cartesianism?

Yes, but why? In the course of reconstituting what we may see as the Lacanian mirror stage of the monkey, Pascal, apologist, thwarted scientist, thwarted rationalist, recognising the face of his hypothesized unbeliever in the Cartesian mirror, plays with it in order to deform and to rebuild it.[28] The paradox is that Cartesian rationalism was supposed to show the futility of rationalism. To perceive this interaction is to apprehend 'différance' in its most modern sense. Pascal skewers the various components of Descartes's philosophy in order to insinuate doubt of its validity and to disparage its intellectual strenuousness. Pascal rewrote the *cogito* to admit tragic vulnerability, just as Lacan rewrote the *cogito* to admit Freud. Descartes's *cogito* is experiential in a special sense. Its identity is ensured by that diamantine guarantee against doubt, the stroboscopic illumination of consciousness. He was the first person writing in French to charge the word 'conscience' with philosophical significance. This animates the dramatic 'I' of his philosophical disquisition who acquires thereby potent intellectual

---

[27] F. A. II , *Méd.* I, pp. 405-406; II, 414, 417; see pp. 423-6 on the wax.

[28] Lacan's exposition of the formative mirror stage is expounded most accessibly in *Ecrits: a Selection* , tr. A. Sheridan (London, 1977), pp. 1-7, reprinted in *Modern Literary Theory: A Reader*, ed. P. Rice and P. Waugh (London, 1989), pp. 122-7.

independence.[29] Descartes's supreme isolation of the self, achieved
through a superb act of will, confers on the 'je' the distinctiveness which
sets him apart from scholasticism, enabling him to tilt Western
philosophy on a dramatically new course. Pascal's contextualisation of
apologetic dialogue in the world of personal experience and of science is
equally novel. Thus the respective *chiquenaudes* of our authors nudge
forward the barriers of Western consciousness.

The 'I' of the *Pensées* at its most moving speaks as a forlorn alien in
a metaphysical world of privation finding no *raison d'être*, ultimately to
be hewn down by the proclaimed unreason of the Fall. Thus is the
cogito charged with limp impotency. It rewrites in the strict
structuralist sense the gripping dramatic presentation of inner
monologue in Descartes's greatest text, the *Méditations* rightly
compared by Spoerri to a cathedral.[30] The Everyman of his apologetic,
voicing his epistemological perplexities, asking fundamental questions
about human origin, identity and purpose re-enacts the enquiry of the
Méditations. Pascal refused to sanction the release from the aqueous
floundering described at the beginning of *Méditation* II, created by the
arterial statement 'je suis, j'existe' which enabled Descartes to rescue the
thinking self, whose existence is guaranteed by God. Instead Pascal
chooses to set man adrift on the ocean of scepticism in an act of
deliberate sabotage wherein his sleight of hand should not detract from
the magnitude of its implications. Equally, Descartes's ponderous tones
should not detract from the magnitude of the revolution he wrought by
positing a solipsistic metaphysics as the basis of all logical enquiry.

Pascal's metaphors consciously buckle the formal railway line of
rationalism, rejecting Porphrys's metaphysical tree. Although the roots
are spurned, the trunk stands. Descartes's questions are retained as
Pascal somersaults from the structuring branches, obliging his seeker
after truth into contortions of the animal machine in order to propose
salvation not in philosophic truth, but in the poetry and unreason of the
Deus absconditus.

We move finally to the fragment 'Disproportion de l'homme' which
compresses the scientific preoccupations of the century into four pages
of brilliant vulgarisation. It situates man between two infinities of
greatness and minuteness, each of which paradoxically dwarfs him, and

---

[29] On the originality of the Cartesian system see *Cahiers de Royaumont*, pp. 100-107. For a recent
defence of his gambit see P. Markie, *Descartes's Gambit* (London, 1986), and of his novel notion of
inference see S. Gaukroger, *Cartesian Logic: an essay on Descartes's conception of inference* (Oxford,
1989), esp. pp. 26-71.

[30] Spoerri, art. cit., p. 278.

maroons him on 'un milieu vaste qui échappe à nos prises, nous glisse et fuit d'une fuite éternelle'. The *milieu* here is physical, whereas that defining human knowledge in both writers was metaphorical. Our being dissolves in liquid alliteration, despite our endeavours to seek a crutch: 'Nous brûlons du désir de trouver une assiette ferme pour y édifier une tour qui s'élève à l'infini, mais tout notre fondement craque et la terre s'ouvre jusqu'aux abîmes.' This image of a disintegrating tower of Babel mocks our *hubris*. While we hanker for infinity, the preposterous and gigantic edifice of our pretentions to build between the finite and the infinite world heaves and subsides. The image evokes an abyss that is both metaphorical and real, that stupefies and dazzles. Demolition threatens our concrete dreams of a secure vantage point from which to survey kaleidoscopic, whirring space as the Cartesian metaphors of architecture crash around us, and the rigid fortification of geometric knowledge caves in. These lines mark deliberate sabotage of the stolid Cartesian house of knowledge, which the philosopher believed himself called upon by God to rebuild from scratch. In part I of the *Discours* he lauds 'la certitude et l'évidence' of men's mathematical reasoning which is rooted in 'fondements si fermes et si solides' (I, 574-5). The prolonged opening comparison of Part II of the *Discours* extols the linear regularity of town planning. Descartes infers that demolition is essential for buildings whose 'fondements n'en sont pas bien fermes' (I, 581). Robustly he claims the right to rebuild his own basic assumptions on the rock of pure logic. His four rules, set out with crisp aridity, imply total congruency between his recurring building metaphors and his analytical method which probes the very essence of mind and matter in order to achieve a coherent understanding of the universe.

Thus, while at first blush it appears true to say that for Pascal metaphor is both affective and paradoxical, while for Descartes it is utilitarian, we cannot rest our case there. In both writers metaphor acts as a truss for a transcendental philosophical framework, transforming man's purchase on mental and corporeal reality. Pascalian metaphor checkmates that of Descartes in major fragments. Yet the formulation of their quest for truth and meaning bears an amazing affinity, and in each the body-mind dichotomy is harnessed to startlingly original effect.

Does then the use of metaphor as the cosh of rationalism in Pascal, the stealthy substitution of one set of rules for another, merely garrot intellectual inquiry in contrast with the quickening intellectual force of Cartesian metaphor at its best? I fear the answer must be at least in part in the affirmative. Pascal uses metaphor as a nuclear warhead with which to penetrate the cocoon of abstraction essential for the elaboration of the Cartesian metaphysic. Goldmann rightly highlights the fundamental truth that man was forbidden to eat of the tree of knowledge in the Old Testament, whereas the whole strategy of Descartes is to encourage us to eat of his tree.[31] Frequently the sleight of hand whereby Pascal reinscribes Cartesian notions into his text conceals murder most foul of the insight of the *Méditations*. At his most daring he converts the automaton into a teleological vehicle for transcendence. In each author metaphor operates meteoric and baffling transmutations of old signs, both in their separate and overlapping spheres, each initiates the first steps towards independent modernism based upon a 'fonds qui est tout à moi' (I, 582). Pascal is at his most innovative as a polemicist when he filches certain basic principles of the Descartes he castigates as 'inutile et incertain et pénible' (fr. 84) in order to utilise them in the quest for the equally hard-won certainty of faith. Perhaps their systems of thought are not quite as irreductible as Spoerri claims, and their metaphors are assuredly less physical than proponents of rhetoric as a simple art of propaganda maintain.[32] Descartes transferred to Pascal a new interpretation of the quicksilver perils and power of consciousness. His machine, triple checked for resistance to ratiocination, is cranked up by his opponent into automatic gear, steering towards a destination that would have irked its creator beyond reason. At the other end of the scale each philosopher employs the idea of infinity to strikingly tendentious and original purpose.

I have stressed that our comparison offers a classic example of post-structuralist Derridean *bricolage*. If we adopt in conclusion Derrida's two powerful alternative paradigms for interpretations of interpretation of meaning, Pascal belongs to the category of those who decipher a truth and a religious origin beyond play, beyond *'divertissement'*.[33] He places us within the context of Christian transcendentalism, where exiled Man on earth endures the wretchedness of a 'roi dépossédé' (fr. 116). Descartes belongs to the second category. He aimed to transcend the play of signs and signifiers on earth in order to restore a reassuring foundation to human existence. This interaction of true minds inscribes moving and exploding geometries on the verge of merging into a novel and shocking architecture. Finally, I submit that if Descartes used metaphor to put a stop to his uncertainties, Pascal used it as a trap to supplement, in the strict post-structuralist sense, or to transfix the splintered Cartesian ego in the black hole of slippery fixed points and quaking configurations of baffling infinities.

---

[31] This is his concluding intervention to the discussion of P. Mesnard's paper, *Cahiers*, p. 359.

[32] Spoerri, p. 287.

[33] See J. Derrida, *Writing and Difference*, tr. A. Bass (London, 1978), pp. 293-5.

Corneille: the spoken and the unspoken

BY

WILLIAM DICKSON

UNIVERSITY OF GLASGOW

In general, criticism of Corneille has emphasised his rhetoric, 'la force des vers' on which the author prided himself in the *Examen* of *Rodogune*. It has been less concerned to tease out the implications of the silences of his characters. His rhetoric is indeed an 'orientation ancienne' of criticism, commented on throughout the seventeenth and eighteenth centuries, notably by Voltaire.[1] But until the work of Fumaroli and Barthes,[2] little has been written on it this century. Their 'orientation moderne' has put language at the very heart of the critical exegesis of his plays. When this approach is extended to include both what is said and what is left unsaid, *le dit et le non-dit*, we are led to question the themes of *gloire* and *devoir*, so often presented as Corneille's ethic and encouraged to interpret the plays as a rhetoric of appearances. Herland has already shown in *Horace* that words and silence are ambivalent and that what is said does not always correspond to what is understood. Characters misunderstand one another, attempt to conceal their emotions, or present themselves as other than they are.[3] Other plays show similar incomprehension and strategies of concealment in the protagonists.

As a dramatist, Corneille was proud of his rhetoric and his technical mastery of language and the alexandrine, of the linguistic *tour de force*. In the course of his work, from the early comedies to the late tragedies, there is a movement from a situation where characters express themselves fully, where the language is developed to the point of ornateness, often with strong literary overtones, to a situation where the

---

[1] Cf. Voltaire, *Commentaires sur Corneille* (1766) and Fontanier, *Les Figures du discours* (1830), which is based largely on the practice of Corneille and Racine.

[2] Cf. R. Barthes, 'L'Ancienne Rhétorique, aide-mémoire', *Communications*, 16 (1970), 172-223; M. Fumaroli, 'Rhétorique et dramaturgie dans *L'Illusion comique* de Corneille', *17e Siècle*, 80-81 (1968), 107-32.

[3] L. Herland: *'Horace' ou la naissance de l'homme*, 1952; see in particular his insistence on the suffering of Horace, pp. 84-7, and his interpretation of the 'mensonge héroïque' of II, ii-iii, pp. 103 - 134.

characters are reluctant to give expression to their emotions, especially in public. As the monologue also became unfashionable (for reasons of *invraisemblance*),[4] complex feelings are often hinted at rather than expressed.[5] Thus we find both silences and scenes or situations in which what the characters say is no longer transparent and requires interpretation by the listener.[6] Characters speak in order to express their thoughts and their emotions or to create a favourable image. As in *L'Illusion comique*, the figure of the playwright is occasionally perceptible behind the characters. Their language evolves in the course of Corneille's career to present an appearance of noble themes while suggesting a different underlying, emotional reality, both to those on stage and the spectators.[7] Ultimately, language conceals rather than conveys information; it deceives others, and creates ambiguity. As the truth is gradually perceived, so dramatic tension is heightened. Just as irony functions on the dual levels of the apparent and the true meaning, so language in Corneille works on two levels. Both convey information and conceal it, appearing to signify one thing but in truth signifying something different. The two levels of language, a variation on *signifiant* and *signifié*, correspond to *être* and *paraître*. It is because of this ambiguity in language that it is dangerous to assume that a character believes completely in what he says.

Some plays give obvious indications of the poet's attitude. After the very literary style of the early comedies, *L'Illusion comique* explicitly shows the verve of the orator and the manipulation by the playwright of both protagonists and spectator. *Suréna*, at the end of Corneille's career, embodies both the temptation and the refusal to speak, and these two irreconcilable tendencies are only resolved in the silence of death. *La Mort de Pompée*, as an example of the plays of the main period, pinpoints the growing discrepancy between the spoken and the unspoken, and the unspoken is perceived by the spectator through gesture. That discrepancy (*écart*) holds the key to our interpretation of

---

[4] J. Scherer, *La Dramaturgie classique*, 1962, pp. 256-60.

[5] Cléopâtre in *Rodogune* is perhaps the most obvious case where a character has kept silent, but is now prepared to reveal herself to a limited extent, according to the circumstances. Séleucus's reply to his mother: 'Le repect me défend d'en dire davantage' (l. 1471) is a clear example of the veiled threat. Antiochus on the other hand refuses to interpret words or events: 'Non, je n'écoute rien [...]' (l. 1767).

[6] Polyeucte is a notable case and gives rise to very different interpretations in consequence. How should the spectator interpret the volte-face of Polyeucte in II, vi? Pauline has enough difficulty discerning his feelings in IV, iii. W.S. Brooks, 'Polyeucte's Martyrdom, "une autre explication" ', in *The Modern Language Review*, LXXII (1977), 802-810 shows the ambiguity of certain key scenes and statements in this respect.

[7] The council scenes of *Cinna* (II, i) and *Sertorius* (III, i) illustrate this. Behind the political arguments, there are unspoken personal motives and emotions.

the characters and the plays, inviting us to view language, not for what it appears to signify, but as a mask requiring interpretation.

Thus, after an initial period in which Corneille glorified linguistic creativity in his comedies, his characters' speech becomes more opaque in the tragedies. If his protagonists search for other meanings, then we the spectators ought to do likewise and refrain from assuming that the major protagonists mean what they say. We ought not to equate public and private persona, 'le paraître et l'être'. Language *may* be a mask, designed to create an image.

Like all the authors of the time, Corneille gives us little in the way of stage directions:

> Curiace va quitter Camille pour aller au combat. Comment Corneille les voyait-il sourire, se serrer, s'éloigner, nous ne le saurons pas. Il n'était d'usage de fournir des indications scéniques que dans les cas d'extrême nécessité [...] Il revient donc au lecteur d'imaginer décors, éclairages, costumes, mouvements scéniques [...] de pratiquer en somme une manière de lecture en relief.[8]

Stage directions are written into the text—'Prends un siège, Cinna' (*Cinna*, 1425)—and indicate changes of mood or gesture: 'Mais courage, il s'émeut, je vois couler des larmes. (*Polyeucte*, 1256). We have to base our interpretations of the characters on what they say in any given situation, and take our cue from what other characters perceive and how they interpret what is said. We may even turn to other plays for guidance in interpreting what is said. It is of course dangerous to interpret one play in the light of another and impose an interpretation which forces all the plays into one framework or dialectic. Yet there is sufficient homogeneity in Corneille's production to justify such cross-interpretation. His fondness for self-quotation shows his awareness of this cross-reference, and he is aware of the effect of the echo on the spectator.

> Je suis maître de moi comme de l'univers [...] (*Cinna*, 1696)

becomes

> Maître de l'univers sans l'être de moi-même [...] (*Tite et Bérénice*, 407)

Self-quotation, even in the form of self-parody, produces this homogeneity, entitling us to relate his plays to one another. Terms such as *gloire* or *devoir* may refer to appearances, not to being (reality). The character may not believe in them but use them as a façade, a

---

[8] G. Couton, *Corneille et la tragédie politique*, 1984 p. 5. Couton is here following the line of criticism first suggested by Herland.

justification or cover for his emotions. Focus on the literal meaning of key terms as opposed to the dramatic situation can mislead us by encouraging us to oversimplify the characters and to expect a facile solution to their dilemmas.[9] Corneille has often suffered at the hands of critics because they fail to read between the lines of his speeches, even when he explicitly invites them so to do.

My starting point is *L'Illusion comique*, because it renders explicit aspects of language which are implicit in earlier plays. Each of the three personages, Alcandre, Matamore and Clindor, embodies a different aspect of language, and the device of the play within the play adds a further dimension to our linguistic awareness. Alcandre is the playwright, showing the role of language in literary creation; Matamore uses language for purposes of escapism, and his verbal exuberance gives rise to fantastic illusion; Clindor shows its ambiguity, as the verb becomes reality; while the play within the play reinforces its opacity, obliging the spectator to reinterpret the whole of the preceding action.

Alcandre, the 'metteur en scène', represents the playwright, when he sets out to 'faire *voir* la fortune éclatante' of Dorante (126)

> ... Je vais de ses amours
> Et de tous ses hasards vous *faire le discours.*
> Toutefois, si votre âme était assez hardie,
> Sous une *illusion* vous pourriez *voir* sa vie [...] (147-50)

Language makes us *see* in our mind's eye or on stage, it is a *representation* which imitates reality, a mimesis. Moreover, Alcandre insists on the role of language as style, as ornament:

> Son style prit après de plus beaux ornements [...] (179)

The play is a poem, recited by the actors, who *appear* to die in a combat of alexandrines, and this evokes pity and sympathy for them in the spectator (1753-7). Pridamant, the father of Clindor, represents the emotional involvement of the spectator, and Alcandre comments on numerous occasions about the emotions he will feel, although often in ambiguous terms (e.g. 215, 621, 977). Alcandre is the public representation of the playwright, responsible through language, through

---

[9] O. Nadal, *Le Sentiment de l'amour dans l'œuvre de Corneille* (Paris, 1948), and especially the *Étude conjointe: de quelques mots de la langue cornélienne ou d'une éthique de la gloire,* show the dangers of this approach. The hair-splitting definitions of *gloire*, for instance, have led to an over-insistence on its role in the psychology of the protagonists.

ornament for the creation of an illusion, a literary artefact, which gives pleasure to the spectator through playing on his emotions.

In the case of Matamore, there are two points to be noted. Firstly, verbal exuberance or linguistic inventiveness,[10] exemplified by the description of the fire which his sword might cause, were he to draw it:

> Oui, mais les feux qu'il jette en sortant de prison
> Auraient en un moment embrasé la maison,
> Dévoré tout à l'heure ardoises et gouttières,
> Faîtes, lattes, chevrons, montants, courbes, filières [...] (747-50)

The exaggeration and technical detail with which the conflagration is evoked constitutes a veritable *tour de force*, compelling us to admire not only Matamore the 'beau parleur', but behind him the poet capable of such linguistic invention and technical mastery. Such a 'morceau de bravoure' in fact reveals the poet who should in theory remain hidden in a drama behind the characters. The effect of the description is calculated to force our admiration or astonishment rather than to provoke comic laughter *per se*.

Secondly, the 'fire' is presented as in a dream, in the conditional tense; in his imaginings, Matamore is incapable of relating words to reality, *signifiant* to *signifié*. What we have is a form of verbal escapism. Reality is transformed through language and metaphor into mythology. Language, the creation of an illusion, replaces reality, and the spectator is invited to perceive the *décalage* or *écart*.[11] Isabelle and Lyse all too easily decode the language of Matamore; for them, 'faire la sentinelle' (1170-3) equals fear, and living on nectar and ambrosia (1181-8) spells hunger. They interpret his words, lest the spectator be deceived by high-flown language. We are not being referred here to the author, as with Alcandre; we are invited to perceive the discrepancy between words and what they signify and Matamore's use of language to escape reality, not to control it.

Clindor takes the theme of illusion and language one stage further. On the one hand, he can adopt the language of Matamore and invent exaggerated tales which will please his master, fully aware of the gap between what he is saying and reality. Hence Clindor is capable of using irony, whereas Matamore is not.

---

[10] Cf. R. Garapon, *La Fantaisie verbale et le comique dans le théâtre français du moyen âge à la fin du 17ème siècle* (Paris, 1957), p. 164: 'le public est beaucoup moins amusé [...] qu'il n'est ravi d'admiration devant une pareille virtuosité verbale'.

[11] R. Barthes, *Le Degré zéro de l'écriture*, 1960, uses the term *écart* for the stylistic difference between a neutral style (the *degré zéro*) and literary expression. The concept is useful not only in stylistics, but also for denoting the discrepancy between *signifiant* and *signifié*, as in this case.

More subtly still, Clindor manipulates the clichés of love in order to make Isabelle fall in love with him, but despite his appropriate use of language, his professed affection is insincere. The proper use of language does not guarantee its veracity: his insincerity is not revealed in what he says or how he acts with Isabelle but only in his parallel courtship of Lyse. In this case, the 'sincerity gap' conceals real deceit, but the hiatus between language and reality is much narrower than the mythological gulf we find in Matamore and it is only brought into the open in subsequent scenes. We find here that ambiguity or duplicity of language which will be developed in later plays in the deception practised by the Machiavellian counsellor and which is based on the gulf between *être* and *paraître*.

If the ultimate criterion of linguistic good faith is to suit word to deed, then Clindor transcends simple deception and achieves this level. He does this firstly with Matamore when he warns him not to court Isabelle in III, ix and secondly, with Adraste. In III, xi, deeds almost literally replace words as Clindor kills Adraste when he is attacked. The verb literally becomes action; words of *bravoure* are replaced by deeds. Clindor foreshadows Rodrigue and the heroes of the tragedies who will suit their actions to their words.

Just as Clindor employs artful language to make Isabelle fall in love with him, so does Lyse when she seduces the gaoler to enable Clindor to regain his freedom. This shows Lyse's acting talents, both in terms of gesture and language, and gives us a first version of a play within the play. We are shown Lyse's conflicting emotions of jealousy and love and prepared for her performance. There is no such preparation in terms of illusion for the play within the play of Act V: as spectators, we assume that we are seeing a truthful representation of events, until Alcandre reveals otherwise. Given the context of Acts II-IV, it is only too plausible to see the play within a play as a repeat performance of infidelity, seduction and revenge, the logical sequence of Clindor's previous conduct. To our surprise, it shows instead the power of dramatic language as illusion, not truth or action. In paralleling and re-enacting reality, the language of Corneille's characters may conceal a totally different reality. The situation dictates the interpretation, not the words. If we take the words at face value, we may come to the wrong conclusions. In the plays which follow, no single character is available to embody the hesitations, silences and comments of Alcandre or offer an authoritative interpretation of events.

In what follows, I shall concentrate on the development of the opacity of language and the gulf between *être* and *paraître*.

The equation between words and deeds indicated in Clindor is achieved in the tragedies of the main period, in Rodrigue, Horace, Auguste and Polyeucte. At the same time, there is an element of ambiguity or duplicity with regard to the expression of emotion, and although the character may try to control it through language, he does not always succeed. In fact, the protagonists often find it easier not to refer to their emotions at all, but their gestures betray what is unuttered. We are moving into a period of illusion and omission, *le non-dit*. It is easier to control the external world, one's situation, than the internal world of one's feelings. In the plays from *Le Cid* through to *La Mort de Pompée* we see the characters' feats of language parallel their feats of arms, but their control of their emotions or inner reality is achieved through the creation of an image or façade which occasionally cracks. However composed Horace may appear to be in his verbal duel with Curiace (II, iii), he appears to Curiace to be in a state of emotional defeat when he appears on stage with Sabine in II, vi. Yet little of this can be deduced from what he himself says. Horace equates words and actions on the surface, but he is no 'surhomme', and his emotional stress in conveyed in comments by others. In the period after 1660, characters find it increasingly difficult to translate words into action, to do what they promise, to create even such a façade as Horace.

The key plays in this respect are *La Mort de Pompée* and *Cinna*, for they both explicitly show the gap between intention and realisation, between image and reality, between *paraître* and *être*.

In *La Mort de Pompée*, the play opens with a council scene deliberating how to receive Pompée. It is decided to receive him, so as to assassinate him. The language of the opening scene is particularly ornate, full of imagery; Corneille speaks of a 'style élevé' and 'des vers pompeux' in his *Examen*. This contrasts strongly with the baseness of the discussion. It illustrates the discrepancy between the level of language and the subject matter, between *forme* and *fond*. This duplicity has a knock-on effect (or one of 'contamination'), perceptible even in César, whose immediate reaction to Pompée's death is closely watched and interpreted by Achorée. He had witnessed Pompée's death earlier and is presented as a reliable eye-witness. He is struck by César's initial failure to react:

> César, à cet aspect, comme frappé du foudre,
> Et comme ne sachant que croire ou que résoudre,
> Immobile, et les yeux sur l'objet attachés,
> Nous tient assez longtemps ses sentiments cachés [...] (769-72)

He highlights the moment of hesitation in César: he conjectures that
César is relieved at first that Pompée is dead, although he attempts to
conceal it, and only then finds the tears and the words which correspond
to the image of dignity, gloire and générosité which he wishes to
convey.

> Il se juge en autrui, se tâte, s'étudie,
> Examine *en secret* sa joie et ses douleurs,
> Les balance, choisit, laisse couler des pleurs;
> Et forçant sa vertu d'être encor la maîtresse,
> *Se montre* généreux par un trait de faiblesse. (782-6)

Corneille invites the audience to see a side of César which will be
concealed subsequently and to be aware that henceforth what we see is
the public façade of a leader conscious of his importance on the world
stage. Even in the scenes with Cléopâtre, we are conscious of someone
performing for an audience, carefully controlling his image, just as
Cléopâtre does. Noble language stylises emotion just as it renders base
deeds acceptable linguistically. Unfortunately for his noble, all-powerful
image, César fails to influence events: Pompée is killed without
reference to him, and his attempts to save Ptolomée fail. César is
perhaps ultimately closer to Matamore than to Clindor! He fails to have
any decisive influence on events, and Achorée unmasks for us
perceptively his exercise in public relations.

Cinna shows clearly how the image or façade is created, how the
spectator is manipulated. It perhaps shows us most clearly the
interaction between public discourse and private thoughts and how the
public persona may differ considerably from the private person. The
best illustration of this is Cinna himself. An excellent orator, he is fully
conscious of the effects of his language. He notes how the conspirators
react to his words:

> Vous eussiez vu leurs yeux s'enflammer de fureur,
> Et dans un même instant, par un effet contraire
> Leur front pâlir d'horreur et rougir de colère. (161-2)

Then he enumerates the means of acting on them by: 'un long récit'
(173), 'je leur fais des tableaux' (177), and 'j'ajoute à ces tableaux la
peinture effroyable [...] ' (189). He emphasises the use of depiction to
drive home his message, the influence of the image on the emotions of
his hearers. And he spells out the effect:

> Mais pourrais-je vous dire à quelle impatience,
> A quels frémissements, à quelle violence,
> Ces indignes trépas, quoique mal figurés,
> Ont porté les esprits de tous nos conjurés?
> Je n'ai point perdu temps, et voyant leur colère,
> Au point de ne rien craindre, en état de tout faire,
> J'ajoute en peu de mots [...] (209-215)

Cinna, the orator, has consciously played on the emotions of his hearers, but without necessarily being emotionally involved himself. In fact, on a second level, his oratorical *tour de force* is designed to impress Émilie favourably by presenting himself in an heroic light. Judging by her *tutoiement* in response, he has succeeded.

Not only is Cinna at one or two removes from the conspiracy, a manipulator rather than a participant, but he appears to lack any moral sense of its implications. To him, justice is not an absolute value. Any moral judgement on the conspiracy is relative, depending on the reactions of Émilie and the populace:

> Demain j'attends la haine ou la faveur des hommes [...]
> Que Rome se déclare ou pour ou contre nous,
> Mourant pour vous servir, tout me semblera doux. (250; 259-60)

Validity is conferred on his action by the people or Émilie. Words and actions are empty and can be adapted or interpreted to fit the situation. What Cinna says does not correspond to his beliefs, if any. This would account for his oratory with Auguste in II, i, when he persuades Auguste to retain the throne in a brilliant *tour de force*, which apparently contradicts his own principles. As such, Maxime finds Cinna's stance incomprehensible (II, ii). Later, Auguste likewise suggests that Cinna's motivation is not principles but personal ambition (1509). It is only in his monologue in III, iii that Cinna appears to begin to think through his position. This is precisely what Auguste seems to recognise when he suggests:

> Apprends à te connaître et descends en toi-même [...] (1517)

Cinna's monologue in III, iii at the very centre of the play underlines the importance of language. It emphasises the manner of presentation, and Cinna for once realises that language cannot solve the dilemma into which he has talked himself:

> Donne un plus *digne nom* au *glorieux* empire
> Du *noble* sentiment que la *vertu* m'inspire,
> Et que l'*honneur* oppose au coup précipité

De mon *ingratitude* et de ma *lâcheté*,
Mais plutôt continue à le *nommer faiblesse*,
Puisqu'il devient si faible auprès d'une maîtresse [...]
Qu'une âme *généreuse* a de peine à *faillir*! (865-70; 875)

For Cinna, the problem is how one equates *signifié* and *signifiant*. Are his feelings to be described honourably ('digne', 'glorieux') or is he a failure ('ingratitude', 'lâcheté', 'faiblesse', etc.)? Cinna's opinion of himself is determined by the terminology, whether he can see himself in positive or negative terms. Image is determined by lexical choice. Or rather, we should speak of Cinna's attempts at creating an image of himself, insofar as he recognises that Émilie's opinion is the determining factor.

Cinna fails to persuade Émilie because he is in love with her and therefore incapable of distancing himself emotionally and exploiting those techniques of visual presentation which were so effective with the conspirators. Instead, he uses rational *sententia* and conjures up a peaceful vision of power under Octave—a blunder in terms of lexical choice. Émilie replies with indignation conveyed in numerous exclamations and sharply formulated lines. It is no surprise that his oratory fails to persuade Émilie, who emphasises the ambiguity of his ethical terminology:

Je fais gloire, pour moi, de cette ignominie,
La perfidie est noble [...] (973-4)

Cinna is not the only character concerned with self-presentation. So is Émilie. A comparison of the first two scenes of the play is instructive in this respect. In I, ii, in her discussion with Fulvie, Émilie sets out her decision to proceed with the assassination of Auguste and uses such terms as liberty and Rome, as well as public recognition for being the inspiration behind the conspiracy (the element of *gloire*). She refuses to acknowledge any debt of gratitude to Auguste for adopting her as his daughter, and points out that she is still 'la fille d'un proscrit'. But the final, weak reason, that it is too late, invalidates by its very emptiness all that precedes it:

Il est tard après tout de m'en vouloir dédire. (137)

If Cinna is killed, she can always follow him in death.

This particular scene, which contains all that is necessary for the exposition, does not resemble the opening monologue, which was omitted for much of the eighteenth century. In the opening scene, Émilie does not mention Rome, gloire or her adoption by Auguste. Her preoccupations are private: witness the vivid if fleeting evocation of her father's death and her lengthy expression of concern for Cinna. The decision at the end is purely emotional, corresponding to the strident tone of the monologue, as evinced in the continual use of apostrophe. In the second scene, which is much calmer in tone, the spectator sees not the private Émilie, but the heroine concerned to create an appropriate image of herself as a youthful, idealistic woman. She constructs her image before the eyes of Fulvie and the spectators by using this opportunity to make her decision public. She cannot go back on a public pronouncement and the public persona then takes over for the rest of the play, apart from a moment's hesitation at the end of III, v, when she almost sends Fulvie to bring back Cinna. Émilie is 'un personnage en quête de son image', but the author varies the style and the figures of speech to indicate the different persona.

Auguste shows more depth than the others. Unconcerned by love, he can concentrate on the real issue of the play, the private person on a public stage, private disillusion contrasting with the façade of power and expressed in the image of:

> Et, monté sur le faîte, il aspire à descendre. (370)

The linguistic contradictions mirror the inner contradictions. Auguste has discovered that self-fulfilment is not to be found in appearances, in externals, in the trappings of power. He is nonetheless persuaded by Cinna to keep the empire, against his better judgment. Lucid though Auguste is, his use of counsellors shows his inability or unwillingness to think through the issue clearly in terms of self-appraisal. True lucidity, self knowledge, comes in stages, firstly with the revelation of the conspiracy in IV, i, followed by the temptation of death in IV, ii, and finally the realisation of the full extent of the conspiracy in V. Only then does he realise his isolation and the fact that he must decide alone, that his problem is purely personal, requiring a personal response. The repeated use of the verb *être*:

> Je suis maître de moi comme de l'univers,
> Je le suis, je veux l'être. Ô siècles, ô mémoire [...] (1696-7)

is an attempt to impose his will on himself, to become what he wants to be, to make being and appearances coincide. He invokes History to fix that instant when he becomes a whole person. In achieving this, he encourages the others to discover the same unity of being at the extreme limit, and turns the energy saved from the conflict within him into positive, outgoing dynamism. His solution is what Émilie has sought throughout, and what Cinna has been aware of since III, iii. The change in him is *visible*. *Être* and *paraître* are united and coincide in 'je le suis, je veux l'être'. It is the extreme point where words are translated into deeds. Action has become more difficult, the moment of hesitation longer, and the instant of transition shorter and more dramatic.

Cinna is a very clear example of the ambiguity of language, of the importance of the theme of *être* and *paraître*, however much it appears to emphasize Roman qualities such as *honneur* or *gloire*. It is made explicit. In the other great plays, the themes of private person and public persona, of hesitation and sudden decisions are also present, but rarely presented as explicitly as in *Cinna* or:

> Va, je ne te hais point. (*Le Cid*, 963)

After *Cinna*, the problem of être and paraître becomes increasingly acute. Characters are increasingly unable to make the grand gesture, to translate words into deeds.

Suréna is the final stage in this development. On the one hand, Suréna and Eurydice love each other, but only confess it to each other after Palmis has served as an interpreter. Their relationship is briefly threatened by the proposed marriage of Suréna to Mandane, when jealousy briefly clouds the understanding of the lovers.

If, for the lovers, *être* and *paraître* coincide after their initial confession, and they can speak of their emotions without concealing them, their love must be concealed from all others, especially Pacorus and the King, Orode. At court, therefore, language becomes opaque; perfectly valid excuses are given which have a certain political validity in order to conceal their love, but these are perceived as untruthful, especially by the perceptive, jealous Pacorus. The play develops into a long interrogation of the lovers, who try to remain silent while the interrogators seek to find out the truth. They succeed in piecing it together by juxtaposing different reactions in different scenes. The situation reveals the truth, which words seek to conceal.

As has been always been the case, emotions cannot be suppressed or transferred on command. Suréna will not marry Mandane, nor Eurydice, Pacorus. They find valid excuses to delay or reject the weddings, for they are incapable of renouncing one another. What we witness is the inability of characters to take decisions which run counter to their emotions and the simultaneous construction of a facade to conceal that emotion. No one is deceived, however.

> L'amour dans sa prudence est toujours indiscret,
> A force de se taire, il trahit son secret [...] (1275-6)

What has changed since *L'Illusion comique* is the gravity of the consequences: whereas Matamore's mythology was perceived as harmless, Suréna's deception leads to death. Whereas in *Horace*, the individual was prepared to sacrifice his life and his happiness for the state, in *Suréna* the individual retains his rights and demands that the state act morally and limit its demands on the individual. Suréna accuses the state of duplicity in its use of language, yet is guilty of the same crime himself.

> Mon vrai crime est ma gloire, et non pas mon amour [...] (1651)

In both *Horace* and *Suréna*, the interests of the state and the individual conflict. In the resolution of the conflict, Horace submits to the demands of the state, although this is no solution to his emotional problem. Suréna refuses to solve his emotional dilemma in this way and is assassinated, and the state is gravely weakened by his death.

From the moment that the lovers confess to one another, there is no going back. Once it is named, confessed, their love takes on its own consistency and reality, like Phèdre's for Hippolyte. Hence there are two languages in the play, the language of truth between the lovers and the language of dissimulation which they use with the state and which is paralleled in the veiled threats of the king. Ultimately, the state will not even accept a façade. It rejects any compromise. The only alternative then is to eliminate both emotion and the language which simultaneously expresses and conceals it: both constitute acts of rebellion against the state. The right to silence and emotion is contrary to the interests of the state and leads to the physical death of the hero and heroine. They no longer have the ability to create an acceptable façade, even to go through with the charade of a royal marriage. Physical actions were easier to perform than emotional sacrifice.

If we cannot change the human condition, because of the primacy of our emotions; if

> ... pour être Romain, je n'en suis pas moins homme. (*Sertorius*, 1194)

then the only solution is the eternal silence of the individual in death, because the only valid values in life are the emotions of the individual:

> Que tout meure avec moi, madame [...] (*Suréna*, 301)

Auguste alone appears to offer a solution, but it is valid only because in his case there is no conflict between love and the state. That is why ultimately *Cinna* is not a tragedy.

If *paraître* and *être* cannot be brought together because of the conflict in the hero between his desires and his situation, then all language can do is create a façade, by making it appear that words are transformed into deeds. The attempt to control or suppress emotions such as love is merely delusion. The hidden result is:

> Toujours aimer, toujours souffrir, toujours mourir. (*Suréna*, 268)

The line encapsulates the ultimate physical and emotional death of a hero who has fought vainly to stifle his love. Happiness and suffering is the hallmark of the human condition, not glory or honour:

> Et le moindre moment d'un bonheur souhaité
> Vaut mieux qu'une si froide et vaine éternité. (*Suréna*, 311-12)

'Toujours par quelque endroit fourbes se laissent prendre': the case of Alceste and his *fourbe*

BY

ROBERT MCBRIDE

UNIVERSITY OF ULSTER

The quotation in the title comes from La Fontaine's fable *Le Loup devenu berger*, in which the wolf profits from the shepherd's repose to don his habit and take his crook. So pleased is he with his disguise that he decides to imitate the shepherd's voice, with disastrous consequences for himself, since his raucous tones betray him at once and lead to his death.[1] Many of the fables describe the dangers latent in deception and illustrate the point of La Rochefoucauld's maxim that 'le vrai moyen d'être trompé, c'est de se croire plus fin que les autres'.[2] In the latter maxim, self-deception precedes self-exposure and dovetails neatly with La Fontaine's fable. Central to Alceste's preoccupations in *Le Misanthrope* is the problem of deception. So much so in fact that his universal indictment of human corruption is fuelled by his *fourbe*, who, he claims, is widely known as such but nonetheless continues to thrive on his roguery. Indeed, far from proving an obstacle, his notorious knavery seems to add impetus to his meteoric ascension in society:

> Nommez-le fourbe, infâme, et scélérat maudit,
> Tout le monde en convient, et nul n'y contredit.
> Cependant sa grimace est par tout bienvenue:
> On l'accueille, on lui rit, partout il s'insinue [...] (135-8)

Alceste personalizes his struggle with social duplicity into a desperate *corps à corps* with his *fourbe* which takes the form of a lawsuit. A figure to whom Alceste devotes at least as much attention in the opening

---

[1] *Fables*, ed. G. Couton (Paris, 1962), III, 3, p. 87.

[2] *Maximes*, ed. J. Truchet (Paris, 1967), No. 127, p. 34.

scene as he does to Célimène (49 lines are related to activities directly or indirectly involving the *fourbe*, 46 to Célimène) seems to me to be worth more than a passing reference, and in consequence in this paper I would like to address myself to three questions: (a) who is this *fourbe*? (b) what light does he shed on Alceste's motivation for his crusade against society's values? and (c) what importance does he have in Molière's comic vision within and without the context of this play?

The *fourbe* does not appear in the play, but it could be said that he exercises a more decisive influence than any of the protagonists over the dénouement. In the opening scene, the spectacle of the rascal's unimpeded climb to social heights so enrages Alceste's sense of justice that it is followed at once by his wish to flee society:

> Et parfois il me prend des mouvements soudains
> De fuir dans un désert l'approche des humains. (143-4)

Philinte appends a lenifying speech to deflect his attention, as he adjures him to be more indulgent to human nature and enjoins on him the necessity of flexibility in social intercourse (145-66). Whereas he doggedly remains on an abstract general level of discussion, Alceste implacably brings the dialogue back to his impending lawsuit, the outcome of which will exemplify the universal rule of justice or perversity. Philinte then shifts the conversation to Alceste's love for Célimène, and the *fourbe* is not mentioned thereafter until the first scene of the final act. There we have the outcome of the lawsuit, in which, according to Alceste, the judges have been hoodwinked by the specious pleas of his adversary, who by an injunction in his own favour had contrived to make Alceste the author of an anonymous political satire of authority, obtaining the support of the influential Oronte.[3] It is

---

[3] Cf. the remarks of Grimarest on Alceste's lines here: 'Les Hypocrites avoient été tellement irrités par le *Tartuffe*, que l'on fit courir dans Paris, un livre terrible, que l'on mettoit sur le compte de Molière pour le perdre. C'est à cette occasion qu'il mit dans le *Misantrope* (sic) les vers suivants':

> Il court parmi le monde un livre abominable,
> Et de qui la lecture est même condamnable,
> Un livre à mériter la dernière rigueur,
> Dont le fourbe a le front de me faire l'Auteur.
> Et là dessus on voit Oronte qui murmure,
> Et tâche méchamment d'apuyer (sic) l'imposture;
> Lui qui d'un honnête homme à la Cour tient le rang [...]
>   *La Vie de M. de Molière*, ed. G. Mongrédien (Paris, 1955), p. 93.

L.-A. Ménard published a manuscript which he entitled *Le Livre abominable de 1665 qui courait en manuscrit sous le nom de Molière comédie politique sur le procès de Fouquet* 2 vols (Paris, 1883).

at this point that the vision of the *désert* of the opening scene
materializes into Alceste's resolve to quit this society of wolves (1521-
4).

It has been suggested by Mesnard that the *fourbe* is both 'une sorte de
double d'Oronte' and a 'réplique aggravée'.[4] The dominating trait in the
foppish sonneteer, however, is vanity not rascality. In his scenes with
Alceste (I, ii; V, ii-iv), he lacks that clear-sighted view of his objectives
and delight in malice which are the outstanding characteristics of
Alceste's *fourbe*. Just as Oronte stands as an example to Alceste of the
overweening self-confidence of society's favourites, so the *fourbe*
appears to him as the representative figure of society's injustice and
corrupt ways. The manner in which he is described by Alceste bears a
striking resemblance in its physical and psychological details to
Tartuffe, 'l'âme de toutes la plus concertée', as well as to his acolytes
such as Don Juan, as he appears in the final act of his play.[5] The
similarities span three areas, namely the vocabulary used to describe the
fourbe, his mastery of the technique of appearances, and his
Machiavellian activities. The term *fourbe* is the generic name applied by
Alceste to his opponent (135, 1504). It happens also to be the name
given to Tartuffe by Damis, (*Le Tartuffe* (1041), Cléante (1699),
Valère (1835)), before the hypocrite is consecrated as 'un fourbe
renommé' by l'Exempt (1923). Alceste's *fourbe* is also described
contemptuously as 'ce pied-plat' (129), a term which Damis uses for
Tartuffe (59).[6] Alceste shows a penchant for terms such as 'franc
scélérat' (124, 1532), 'scélérat maudit' (135), which reminds us of
Molière's interpolated stage-note during the hypocrite's second scene
with Elmire: '*C'est un scélérat qui parle*' (1487).[7] 'Traître' is another

---

This is the anonymous *Innocence persécutée*. Ménard believed Molière to be its author, but this is now
generally discounted (see F. Marcus, ' "L'Innocence persécutée" (c. 1665), One Polemicist's Perception
of Contemporary Politics', *Seventeenth-Century French Studies*, 13 (1991), pp. 71-89). Having read
the latter's excellent study of the work (unpublished Ph.D. thesis, University of London, 1985), I share
her view that Molière cannot be seriously considered as its author.

[4] '*Le Misanthrope*: mise en question de l'art de plaire', *Revue d'histoire littéraire de la France*,
LXXII, 5-6 (1972), (pp. 871-2).

[5] This description of Panulphe as he was called in the second version of Molière's play (1667) is
from the *Lettre sur la comédie de l'Imposteur* (20 August 1667), in *Œuvres complètes* of Molière, ed.
G. Couton (Paris, 1971), I, p. 1157. As G. Ferreyrolles observes, 'Tartuffe ressemble comme un frère
au "franc scélérat" avec qui Alceste est en procès', *Molière: Tartuffe* (Paris, 1987), p.103.

[6] A. Furetière in his *Dictionnaire Universel* (1690) defines the term as follows: '*Pied-plat*; on
appelle pied plat, un rustre, un homme de rien qui a des souliers tout unis, et tout plats, comme en
portent ordinairement les païsans'.

[7] Cf. Molière's description of his careful presentation of his hypocrite, in the *Préface* of 1669 to *Le
Tartuffe*: '[...] j'ai mis tout l'art et tous les soins qu'il m'a été possible pour bien distinguer le

favourite term in Alceste's vocabulary (125, 1493), one which Orgon applies to his erstwhile idol Tartuffe (1586) once he is enlightened about him. The *fourbe* is first and foremost a dissembler, whose disguise Alceste pierces at once: 'au travers de son masque on voit à plein le traître' (125). His nauseating grimaces afford him access to high society (137) and are supplemented by the way he rolls his eyes and adopts a mealy-mouthed tone (127), enabling him to triumph legally and socially in despite of reason and morality (1496-7). To Orgon, who extols the saintly virtues of Tartuffe, Cléante depicts hypocritical piety in terms similar to those employed by Alceste about his *fourbe*. He is in no way duped by the pious show of 'façonniers' (325) of Tartuffian ilk, with their 'sacrilège et trompeuse grimace' (362, cf. 330) and 'vaines simagrées' (321), still less by the 'faux clins d'yeux' and the 'élans affectés' (368), the soulful sighing, fervent prayer and wheedling humility which so impressed Orgon as he watched the fraudulent devotions and ostentatious almsgiving of Tartuffe in church (285-8, 293-8). Cléante therefore insists all the more strenuously on the distinction between the mask and the face (331 ff.). Similarly, Dom Juan came to prize the performance of the 'grimaciers' who excel in making such play with 'un soupir mortifié et deux roulements d'yeux' and 'quelque baissement de tête', by means of which they induce people to overlook their immoral behaviour, so maintaining their credit in society's eyes (*Dom Juan*, V, ii).

It is the supreme ability of the *fourbe*, in general, to manipulate appearances so that falsehood not only masquerades as truth but carries greater conviction in the eyes of the onlooker, which constitutes his real achievement. Alceste's *fourbe* triumphs on account of the connivence of the judges whom he has suborned, even succeeding in enlisting the support of Oronte, 'Lui, qui d'un honnête homme à la cour tient le rang' (1507) and the rest of the cabal (1556). Thus does the *fourbe* unite behind him lawgiver, 'honnête homme' and hypocrites in an unlikely and unholy triumvirate. A further refinement, which the stupefied Alceste comes close to admiring for its sheer brazenness, consists in the slanderous attribution of potentially damaging satire to himself by the *fourbe* (1500ff.). Tartuffe makes brilliant pantomimic play with appearances to procure Damis's *donation* (III, vii) as well as the secret papers relating to Orgon's friend Argas which Orgon gave to the hypocrite (V, i). As with Alceste, so the *fourbe* Tartuffe goes to the king with slanderous accusations of a politically compromising nature (1921). Behind Tartuffe (and Dom Juan) stand the resources of the

---

personnage de l'hypocrite d'avec celui du vrai dévot. J'ai employé pour cela deux actes entiers à préparer la venue de mon scélérat', ed. cit., I , p. 884.

omnipresent but invisible cabal, of which we have a glimpse in the oleaginous M. Loyal (*Le Tartuffe*, V, iv), as well as in Philinte's warning against inactivity on Alceste's part regarding his lawsuit:

> Votre partie est forte,
> Et peut, par sa cabale, entraîner [...] (193-4)

and in his concession to Alceste's damning indictment of society: 'Tout marche par cabale et par pur intérêt' (1556). It is clear that Alceste's *fourbe* is not portrayed by him overtly as a religious hypocrite, but as a hypocrite who is prepared to use social and political opportunism to further his own worldly ends. (It should be appended that he would be exceedingly likely to use religious hypocrisy *le cas échéant*, but the ends are just as temporal and materialistic as those of Tartuffe.) In Orgon's home, Alceste's *fourbe* would have adapted his means to the mania of his dupe. In the charmed society of the court, his performance is more uniformly smooth and polished than that of Tartuffe, whose rustic origins he shares.[8] It is also clear that his confident manipulation of others is due in no small measure to the knowledge that he can rely on a network of influential friends to ease his passage to the glittering prizes of society. Alceste's *fourbe* is a secular version of Tartuffe or even Tartuffe in secular guise, prior to, or after, his spell in prison at the expense of the 'Prince ennemi de la fraude' (*Le Tartuffe*, 1906).[9]

The presence of the *fourbe* in Alceste's life helps us to understand something of his motives in pitting himself against society's practices. He wishes us to take him at his face value, as a victim of society's nefarious ways, thwarted in his noble aspiration towards personal and collective probity:

> Je veux qu'on soit sincère, et qu'en homme d'honneur
> On ne lâche aucun mot qui ne parte du cœur. (35-6)

In consequence of his own self-evaluation, it is logical for him to opine that the triumph of his *fourbe* in his lawsuit should stand:

---

[8] See *Le Misanthrope*, 1. 129, and note 6 above. Also Dorine's jibes on Tartuffe's lowly social origins as she tries to jolt Mariane into a reconciliation with Valère, *Le Tartuffe*, 636-48, 656-67.

[9] The Panulphe of the second version of August 1667 (*L'Imposteur*), was also consigned to prison. We do not know if this was his fate in the first completed versions in five acts of the play, presented on 29 November 1664 and 8 November 1665, both of which antedate *Le Misanthrope* (1666) and were performed at Le Raincy for the Prince de Condé, see the *Registre* of La Grange in G. Mongrédien, *Molière recueil des textes et des documents du XVIIe siècle* (Paris, 1973), I, pp. 229, 249.

Comme une marque insigne, un fameux témoignage
De la méchanceté des hommes de notre âge. (1545-6)

In the context of Alceste's unabashed self-recommendation, however, it is judicious to recall La Rochefoucauld's maxim to the effect that 'Dans toutes les professions chacun affecte une mine et un extérieur pour paraître ce qu'il veut qu'on le croie. Ainsi on peut dire que le monde n'est composé que de mines'.[10] An idealist may wear a mask just as well as a *fourbe*. Alceste's extreme expressions of vituperation, his vindictive wish to demolish his *fourbe*, originate from the same source as his antagonism to the customs of polite society — temperamental antipathy.[11] His aggressive stance is responsible for a goodly part of his troubles, as Philinte anticipates in the first scene (182-4) and confirms in Act V, scene i (1525-30). He may attract our sympathy for his idealism, but he is altogether too immoderate. Being every whit as self-interested as those society figures he stigmatizes, he is too volatile to be able to parade as society's innocent victim. He relishes personalized combat with his *fourbe*, and enjoys deflating the pretensions of the members of Célimène's salon, see his clinical character assassination of Clitandre in front of her (475-88). His reaction to the loss of his lawsuit is that of someone who luxuriates in self-flagellation for his self-interest:

... pour vingt mille francs j'aurai droit de pester
Contre l'iniquité de la nature humaine. (1548-9)

At once martyr and iconoclast, he pursues his course with one eye on the history-books and the other on the immediate exhilaration to be gained from knocking down figures of society.

And yet in spite of all Alceste's rodomontades, his fate does not leave us as indifferent as does that of Sganarelle and Arnolphe of *L'École des maris* and *L'École des femmes* respectively. The valedictory misogynist philippic of the former and the deflated expostulation 'Ouf' of the latter possess a different tonality to the bitter-sweet ending of this play.[12] Philinte does concede that a notable, if temporary, miscarriage of justice has occurred (1538-40). The promise of retribution for *fourbes* held out in La Fontaine's fable has not materialized in this case, in spite of all

---

[10] No. 256, ed. cit., p. 66. 'Profession' is defined as 'condition, manière d'être habituelle', ed. cit., p. 644.

[11] See Alceste 89-90, Philinte 97-100 and 105-106.

[12] The editions of *L'École des femmes* published during Molière's life-time print 'Oh' but we know that the original version had 'Ouf' from E. Boursault's *Le Portrait du peintre*, 1664, sc. ii.

Philinte's attempts to modulate Alceste's grievances. Unlike the dénouements to *Le Tartuffe* and *Dom Juan*, no *deus ex machina* intervenes to restore a sense of justice. Philinte and Éliante provide a less absolute and more human alternative, as they set out to change the misanthropist's mind.

Nevertheless, in my view, the ending of *Le Misanthrope* differs only in appearances from the two plays mentioned. In *Le Tartuffe*, the *deus* intervenes with poetic justice to apportion punishment to the hypocrite. In *Dom Juan*, the audience expects the hero to be crushed by the statue, in conformity to the traditional ending inherited by Molière. In both plays, the dénouement is theatrically appropriate and spectacular, but sits uneasily with the psychology of the characters and dramatic momentum. Whereas the *Écoles* end on a comic note of self-deflation deserved and achieved, the three later plays reflect comedy taking place within a sceptical vision of things in which rewards and punishment do not necessarily go to those who merit them. I would like to illustrate this shift in Molière's comic vision with reference to the remarkable *Lettre sur la comédie de L'Imposteur* of August 1667, written to defend the moral standing of the second version of Molière's most controversial play. The writer grounds his justification of the play's morality on an elaborate argument designed to prove the same point that La Fontaine adduces as the lesson from his fable. Nature, or 'la providence de la nature' equips us to discern the reasonable from the unreasonable in human behaviour. The perception of what is ridiculous stems from unreasonable actions, for which we experience contempt. *Convenance* or congruity, characterizes reasonable behaviour, as its opposite, *disconvenance*, or incongruity, designates unreasonable behaviour. The essence of the ridiculous is located in that *disconvenance* between appearances and reality, by virtue of which we laugh at Panulphe.[13] The central passage argues that what is immoral is invariably perceived and exposed as ridiculous: 'La raison de cela c'est que si le ridicule consiste dans quelque disconvenance, il s'ensuit que tout mensonge, déguisement, dissimulation, toute apparence différente du fond, enfin toute contrariété entre actions qui procèdent d'un même principe, est essentiellement ridicule'.[14] This principle is rooted in the moral premise implanted by nature in our minds: 'que la providence de la nature a voulu que tout ce qui est méchant eût quelque degré de

---

[13] Ed. cit., I, p. 1174.
[14] Ibid., p. 1178.

ridicule'.[15] In *Le Tartuffe*, Cléante claims to be able to distinguish true from false piety on the basis of his criterion which he terms variously 'la juste nature' (340) and 'la droite raison' (1609). The ordered view of right and wrong held by the author of the *Lettre* and by Cléante is rendered less simple and efficacious in practice, as two examples from that play demonstrate: (a) When Damis discovers Tartuffe in amorous dalliance with Elmire (III, iv) the hypocrite is able to turn an unpromising situation to his own advantage by inverting the moral principle of 'la vertu raisonnable' and 'le vice déraisonnable'. He knows that the key to his continued ascendancy over the household lies in his manipulation of the domestic despot Orgon. Consequently, his melodramatic performance in which he plangently confesses himself a gross sinner in unspecified and vague terms (1074 ff.), is designed to gull no-one but Orgon, and he is rewarded by the latter's positive encouragement to him to have unrestricted access to his wife. That his performance is directed towards his dupe is to be seen from the manner in which he knowingly overplays his part to suit Orgon's temperamental need for theatrical gesture, as La Bruyère singularly failed to see in his partial correction of Molière's hypocrite in his portrait of Onuphre.[16] (b) Tartuffe's acting style changes radically when, having accepted that part of the inheritance accruing to Damis, Cléante taxes him with conduct unbecoming to a Christian (IV, i). The hypocrite's reply, to the effect that whereas he forgives Damis's immoderate use of language, heaven's interest forbids him to restore the inheritance since it may fall into evil hands, is in no way designed to convince his interlocutor. If Cléante sees through its specious plausibility, the unconcerned Tartuffe eludes his moral arguments effortlessly by means of the pretext of pressing religious duty in the evasive manner described in the *Lettre sur la comédie de l'Imposteur*:

> Enfin la manière dont il met fin à la conversation est un bel exemple de l'irraisonnabilité, pour ainsi dire, de ces bons messieurs, de qui on ne tire

---

[15] Ibid., p. 1178. The letter's analysis of the ridiculous has sometimes been viewed as a purely intellectual one. The theory of the ridiculous is set firmly within a conception of morality based on reason. See E. James who contends, rightly in my view, that its argument is presented within a moral and satirical framework, see 'Molière Moralized: the *Lettre sur la comédie de l'Imposteur*', *Seventeenth-Century French Studies*, XIII (1991), pp. 105-13.

[16] La Bruyère begins his portrait of Onuphre by appearing to criticize the manner in which Tartuffe overplays his role with his dramatic gestures in front of Dorine (III, ii), but then sees the need for his own hypocrite to adapt his acting to his audience: 'S'il marche par la ville, et qu'il découvre de loin un homme devant qui il est nécessaire qu'il soit dévot, les yeux baissés, la démarche lente et modeste, l'air recueilli lui sont familiers: il joue son rôle. S'il entre dans une église, il observe d'abord de qui il peut être vu; et selon la découverte qu'il vient de faire, il se met à genoux et prie, ou il ne songe ni à se mettre à genoux ni à prier', *Les Caractères*, ed. R. Garapon (Paris, 1962), p. 407.

jamais rien en raisonnant, qui n'expliquent point les motifs de leur conduite, de peur de faire tort à leur dignité par cette espèce de soumission, et qui, par une exacte connaissance de la nature de leur intérêt, ne veulent jamais agir que par l'autorité seule que leur donne l'opinion qu'on a de leur vertu.[17]

Pretence, designed to deceive or simply to keep the onlooker at one remove from the truth, is successfully implemented in both cases and evidences a perfect *convenance* between ends and means on the part of the scoundrel.

Tartuffe is essentially a practitioner rather than a theoretician of religious hypocrisy. It could not be otherwise in view of his physical appearance: 'Gros et gras, le teint frais, et la bouche vermeille' as Dorine describes him to Cléante (234). His libidinous temperament impels him towards immediate gratification of his senses, witness the speed with which he proceeds to examine the material of Elmire's dress (III, iii). Dom Juan, on the other hand, takes delight in the preparation of seduction, the strategy of his amorous campaigns affording him an intellectual and aesthetic enjoyment unknown to *fourbes* who are merely *roturiers*. His aristocratic nature is drawn to the rare quality of privilege inherent in 'l'impunité souveraine' (V, ii), which among all vices religious hypocrisy alone confers and for which he provides a kind of conceptual framework and philosophy unattainable to plebeian *fourbes*.

Two reasons, the first utilitarian, the second psychological in nature, serve to reinforce its esoteric appeal for him. The existence of a cabal ready to mobilize its resources should one of its members happen to be exposed and brought to justice renders the prospect of the sovereign exercise of desire irresistible: 'Que si je viens à être découvert, je verrai, sans me remuer, prendre mes intérêts à toute la cabale, et je serai défendu par elle envers et contre tous' (V, ii).[18] The *Lettre* extends this view of the impenetrable network, monolithic self-support and

---

[17] Ed. cit., p. 1161.

[18] Through Dom Juan's use of paradox, P. Dandrey ('*Le Dom Juan* de Molière et la tradition de l'éloge paradoxal', *XVIIe Siècle*, 172, 3 (1991), p. 215) discerns Molière's own attitude towards religious hypocrisy: 'A croire que Molière trouve refuge dans une attitude paradoxale et provocatrice face à l'effondrement des valeurs dont la plus forte, la religion, se trouve minée par une imitation dérisoire et inexpugnable. Le paradoxe ici semble servir de masque élegant à un sceptisme découragé, en même temps qu'il canalise et détourne l'indignation qui risque de la priver de ce détachement hautain et désabusé auquel doit tendre le moraliste lucide. Molière ne se prive pas en tout cas d'y blâmer impitoyablement une société qui ne vaut guère mieux que le rebelle auquel elle offre les armes du mensonge et du masque. Il force ainsi chacun à voir ce que tout le monde feint d'ignorer ou se refuse à regarder—que, s'il est des libertins tapageurs qui sont de méchantes gens, il n'est pas moins de chrétiens par politique ou de dévots fanatiques qui sont les uns d'honnêtes fripons, les autres de redoutables complices des premiers'.

unaccountable activities of religious hypocrites: '[...] qui sont liés
ensemble bien plus étroitement que ne le sont les gens de bien, parce
qu'étant plus intéressés, ils considèrent davantage et connaissent mieux
combien ils se peuvent être utiles les uns aux autres dans les occasions,
ce qui est l'âme de la cabale'.[19] The second reason given by the Dom
resides in the unerring primacy of appearances over fact for humans, by
virtue of which to be seen through or detected by others is a matter of
as much indifference and as little concern to him and his fellow
hypocrites as it is to Tartuffe or Alceste's *fourbe*: 'On a beau savoir
leurs intrigues et les connaître pour ce qu'ils sont, ils ne laissent pas
pour cela d'être en crédit parmi les gens' (V, ii). There are two ways in
which the primacy of appearances creates such a closely-knit web of
pretence that the collective consciousness is unwilling or unable to see
through it. The first consists in the reliance of the *fourbe* on the mental
torpor of his dupes, (who comprise the vast majority of people), by
which the latter are unable or unwilling to prefer the evidence of their
reason to their senses, or as the *Lettre* phrases it: 'parce que les hommes
jugent des choses plus par les yeux que par la raison'.[20] The *fourbe* is
thus conveniently provided with a ready-made form of insurance against
discovery. The second way consists in so concertedly and brazenly
maintaining the fiction of unimpeachable appearances in the face of
detection, whether by Cléante, the family of Orgon, Dom Carlos (*Dom
Juan* (V, iii)) or Alceste, that the moral superiority of the exposer is
blunted and neutralized. It is precisely at this point that even the author
of the *Lettre*, whose abhorrence of hypocrisy in all its forms is
manifest, comes close to admiring the matchless self-control exhibited
by its practitioners under the most extreme pressure: 'Et c'est où il faut
reconnaître le suprême caractère de cette sorte de gens, de ne se
démentir quoi qui arrive, de soutenir à force d'impudence toutes les
attaques de la fortune, n'avouer jamais avoir tort, détourner les choses
avec le plus d'adresse qu'il se peut, mais toujours avec toute l'assurance

---

[19] Ed. cit., p. 1167.

[20] Ed. cit., p. 1164. Earlier, the writer makes the same point when discussing the hypocrite's use
of religious language: '[...] le peuple que ces gens-là (les hypocrites) ont en vue, et sur qui les paroles
peuvent tout, se préviendra toujours d'une opinion de sainteté et de vertu pour les gens qu'il verra parler
ce langage, comme si accoutumés aux choses spirituelles, et si peu à celles du monde [...]', ed. cit., p.
1158. Cf. the lines of William Blake:

> This Life's dim Windows of the Soul
> Distorts the Heavens from Pole to Pole,
> And leads you to believe a lie,
> When you see with, not through, the eye.

The Everlasting Gospel, in *Complete Writings*, ed. G. Keynes (Oxford, 1966), p. 753.

imaginable [...]'[21] The implacable refusal to concede *to any degree
whatsoever* that appearances are appearances or to circumscribe
powerful appetites and worldly ambitions for a moment *even when
detected*, ensures invulnerability for the consummate practitioners of
evildoing:

> ... Plate sin with gold,
> And the strong lance of justice hurtless breaks;
> Arm it in rags, a pigmy's straw doth pierce it.[22]

    Society therefore has ultimately no protection against unscrupulous,
brilliant manipulators of appearances. Its members are either blinded by
dazzling mastery of *jeu de théâtre* and legerdemain, as are Orgon, the
father of Dom Juan, Dom Louis, and Sganarelle, or unable to break
down the carefully layered walls of impenitent and persistent
dissimulation which frustrate definitive exposure and retribution, as are
Cléante, Dom Carlos, Elvire, Alceste. So when Damis fulminates against
the monumental injustice by which his detection of the hypocrite's
adulterous proposition to Elmire leads to his own eviction from his
home (*Le Tartuffe*, III, vi), and Alceste incredulously says of his *fourbe*

> Le poids de sa grimace, où brille l'artifice
> Renverse le bon droit, et tourne la justice! (1497-8)

both are correct in their revulsion at the moral paradox involved but
wrong and immature to think it in any way surprising. They are wrong
because such paradoxes have become the warp and woof of life, as
Elmire well knows, thus retaining her poise in the face of Tartuffe's
felony and her husband's connivence in it (*Le Tartuffe*, 1029-34, 1067-
72) and because, as Philinte points out:

> Ce n'est plus que la ruse aujourd'hui qui l'emporte,
> Et les hommes devraient être faits d'autre sorte. (1557-8)

On account of the hiatus between the way phenomena appear and their
reality and our inability to make the two coincide, it is fallacious
invariably to expect perfect justice from the imperfect humans who
frame it. In the *Pensées*, Pascal sees the authority of lawyers and doctors

---

[21] Ed. cit., p. 1164.

[22] Shakespeare, *King Lear*, IV, vi.

as established and maintained in the mind of the public 'par grimace'.[23]
He who has justice in his favour is he who has the strongest appearances
of justice: '[...] ne pouvant faire que ce qui est juste fût fort, on a fait
que ce qui est fort fût juste'.[24] Or as Alceste shouts from the rooftops
'J'ai pour moi la justice, et je perds mon procès!' (1492)

Alceste's response to the triumph of his *fourbe* however is not the last
word. Were that so, the ending would offer the same kind of bleak
outlook on existence as a Beckett play. Philinte's reaction is to find in
such a reversal 'des moyens d'exercer notre philosophie' (1562). What
at first sight might seem to be a piece of bland moralizing is on
reflection an injunction of much greater value. It is in fact an invitation
to place life in a perspective in which events are seen as possessing
relative and not absolute significance. Such a perspective, nourished by
a continual view of human imperfection and injustice, is yet able to
survive unscathed because it accepts them as part of the human condition
and spectacle. In this spectacle, as Molière well saw in choosing his two
principal characters, the Alcestes of this world need continually to be
reminded of one fact, which Philinte has unavailingly tried to enjoin on
his friend from the opening scene and which he doubtless hurries off to
urge on him yet again at the end: namely, that *fourbes* may come and
fourbes may go, but the comic vision, 'the pure sense of life' rooted in
the rhythms of our existence, goes on forever.[25]

---

[23]*Pensées, Œuvres complètes*, ed. L. Lafuma (Paris, 1963), fr. 44, p. 505. As Pascal also
perceived in the same fragment, authority may also be wielded through astute working on the
imagination of the passions, 'les seuls orateurs qui persuadent toujours', according to La
Rochefoucauld, ed. cit., No. 8, p. 9.

[24] Ed. cit., No. 103, p. 512.

[25] S. Langer, 'The Comic Rhythm', in *Comedy: Meaning and Form*, ed. R.W. Corrigan,
(Pennsylvania, 1969), p. 123. At the outset of the play, Philinte has already attempted to bring the
self-detachment of the comic vision to bear on Alceste's wish to sever all communication with his
fellows:

> Ce chagrin philosophe est un peu trop sauvage,
> Je ris des noirs accès où je vous envisage,
> Et crois voir en nous deux, sous mêmes soins nourris,
> Ces deux frères que peint *L'École des maris* [...] (97-101).

The Celebration of Carnival
in Molière-Lully's
Les Amants magnifiques

ST EDMUND HALL, OXFORD

> Comme voici le *Carnaval,*
> Un *Divertissement royal*
> A présent notre *cour* occupe.
> (Robinet, February 1670)[1]

It is a commonplace that an interpretation of a play should take account of how that play works on stage; yet this simple idea has had almost no impact on the critical study of Molière's *comédies-ballets.* The reason is obvious: we cannot easily judge the theatrical impact of works which are not performed. The few musical works of Molière which do hold a place in the repertoire—*George Dandin, Le Bourgeois gentilhomme, Le Malade imaginaire* —are invariably played in truncated versions which obscure the structural importance of music within them. The result is that critics have mostly failed to come to terms with the aesthetic of the *comédie-ballet,* misunderstanding in the process about one third of Molière's entire *œuvre.*

The growing interest in French baroque music has encouraged more performances of the music of, among others, Lully and Charpentier; in this way, musicologists and producers are uncovering important new directions for literary critics interested in the *comédies-ballets.* The missing parts of Charpentier's score for *Le Malade imaginaire,* for example, were discovered as recently as the 1980s, and Jean-Marie Villégier's production in 1990 (conducted by William Christie)

---

[1] Robinet, 'Lettre en vers à Madame' (8 février 1670), quoted in *Œuvres de Molière,* ed. E. Despois and P. Mesnard, 11 vols (Paris, 1873-1893), VII (1882), p. 353. The text of *Les Amants magnifiques* is quoted throughout from this edition.

provided the first opportunity since 1673 to see and hear the work performed complete.[2]

If this production showed an apparently familiar work in an entirely unfamiliar guise, the 1988 production of *Les Amants magnifiques* by Jean-Luc Paliès came as a revelation of an almost unknown work.[3] The Limoges-based Compagnie Fiévet-Paliès brought the production to Paris to the Théâtre de l'Athénée, in February 1989, to the considerable acclaim of critics (including one from *Opéra International*). Opportunities to see *Les Amants magnifiques* performed complete have been rare indeed. After the initial Court performances in 1670, it was not performed again until 1688, when it was given at the Guénégaud theatre. Thereafter the work received only sporadic performances up to 1694, and it is not clear that these included the *intermèdes*. Certainly, when the piece was next given in Paris, in July 1704, the prologue and *intermèdes* were entirely rewritten by Dancourt, so that from this early date the integrity of Molière's text was crucially compromised.[4]

The 1989 performances of *Les Amants magnifiques* were the first in Paris since a 1954 production at the Comédie Française, and this, though more lavish, had made extensive changes to the *intermèdes*, thereby obscuring the balance between the verbal and musical components. Paliès, on the other hand, chose to present the *comédie-ballet* as Molière and Lully conceived it, with all six *intermèdes* in place, and with all the music. His forces were small — six instrumentalists, two dancers — and could only hint at the full visual and musical splendour of the *comédie-ballet*. By presenting the work entire, however, the production did successfully demonstrate its complex musical-dramatic structure.

Described by one writer as 'la plus méconnue et la plus oubliée sans doute des œuvres de Molière',[5] *Les Amants magnifiques* has shared the fate of other *comédies-ballets* in being dismissed as an incidental, and

[2] See my articles 'Molière-Charpentier's *Le Malade imaginaire*: the first *opéra-comique?*', forthcoming in *Forum for Modern Language Studies*; and 'The Play of Words and Music in Molière-Charpentier's *Le Malade imaginaire*', forthcoming in *French Studies*.

[3] A number of *L'Avant-Scène Théâtre* (No. 845, 1 March 1989) is devoted to this production of *Les Amants magnifiques*, and contains numerous photographs. The production is reviewed by M. Servin in *Les Temps modernes*, No. 512, 44 (1989), pp. 167-72. Extracts from Lully's music for this work are included on a disc recorded in 1988, 'Lully-Molière: les comédies-ballets', cond. M. Minkowski (Erato, ECD 75361).

[4] F.C. Dancourt, *Nouveau Prologue et nouveaux divertissemens pour la comedie des Amans magnifiques* (Paris, 1704). Dancourt's version, which was given eleven performances, was not revived; see A. Blanc, *F.C. Dancourt (1661-1725): la comédie française à l'heure du soleil couchant* (Tübingen, 1984), pp. 94-5.

[5] P. Beaussant, *Lully ou le musicien du Soleil* (Paris, 1992), p. 367.

therefore insignificant work: as recently as 1979, one critic wrote that
'[Molière] n'attacha d'ailleurs guère d'importance à cette petite œuvre
de circonstance; il ne la reprit pas au Palais-Royal et ne la livra pas à
l'impression'.[6] Yet Pellisson long ago pointed out that the Palais-Royal
was not at that time equipped with the machinery necessary to perform
the work, and that Molière may well have chosen not to publish it in
order to prevent it from falling into the public domain.[7]

A second, and more significant criticism often levelled at the
comédies-ballets is that they are disjointed and poorly structured, a view
which has provoked an over-reaction on the part of some critics, who
have gone to lengths to stress their unity: 'Œuvre mineure peut-être',
asserts Guicharnaud, 'Les Amants magnifiques sont néanmoins marqués
par une définitive cohérence dans la conception d'ensemble'.[8] A major
difficulty with this interpretation, however, is that it does not reflect
our response as spectators. In the recent Paris production, the tense
contrasts of the various elements were startling, and it may be more
fruitful to take these as a starting-point and, by describing the function
of these tensions, to show how they help generate the work's dramatic
charge.

A focal point for the tensions of Les Amants magnifiques may be
found in the way in which it exploits, celebrates even, the notion of
carnival, and Bakhtin's discussion of the carnivalesque throws a
revealing light on its alleged incoherences.[9] Carnival is at the origin of
Les Amants magnifiques: ordered by the King as an entertainment for
the Court during the pre-Lenten period of Carnival, the piece was first
performed at Saint-Germain-en-Laye in February, 1670, as part of the
Divertissement royal. The Church had long been attempting to check the

---

[6] G. Mongrédien (ed.), Molière, Œuvres complètes, Vol. IV (Paris, 1979), p. 18.

[7] M. Pellisson, Les Comédies-ballets de Molière (Paris, 1914), pp. 31-33.

[8] 'Les Trois Niveaux critiques des Amants magnifiques', in Molière: Stage and Study: essays in
honour of W. G. Moore, ed. W.D. Howarth and M. Thomas (Oxford, 1973), pp. 21-42 (p. 40); the
same tendency to emphasise the coherence of the comédies-ballets (though he does not discuss Les
Amants magnifiques) is evident in C. Abraham's On the Structure of Molière's Comédies-ballets
(Paris, 1984); R. McBride, in his more wide-ranging study, considers Les Amants magnifiques along
broadly similar lines: 'With sole responsibility for the ballet and comedy, Molière integrates them to
form a unified comedy-ballet' (The Triumph of Ballet in Molière's Theatre (Lewiston-Queenston-
Lampeter, 1992), p. 226).

[9] T. Malachy's Molière: les métamorphoses du carnaval (Paris, 1987) is, though in many ways an
unsatisfactory work, the only extended Bakhtinian study of Molière; it makes no mention of Les
Amants magnifiques.

excesses of carnival,[10] and as the folk culture which supported it went into decline in the course of the seventeenth century, the royal bureaucracy also strove to suppress what it saw as the disruptive forces of festivity.[11] Meanwhile the medieval *fête des fous* had become transmuted into the more sophisticated celebration of carnival,[12] and it was, paradoxically, in the monarch's own Court festivities that the spirit of carnival, albeit in an adulterated form, survived longest:

> Beginning with the seventeenth century, folk-carnival life is on the wane: it almost loses touch with communal performance, its specific weight in the life of people is sharply reduced, its forms are impoverished, made petty and less complex. As early as the Renaissance a *festive court masquerade* culture begins to develop, having absorbed into itself a whole series of carnivalistic forms and symbols (mostly of an externally decorative sort).[13]

It is, Bakhtin argues, through the medium of literature that carnival survives, long after its decline as a social fact: 'We are calling this transposition of carnival into the language of literature the carnivalization of literature'.[14]

Molière is singled out by Bakhtin as an instance of this phenomenon:

> The contents of the carnival-grotesque element, its artistic, heuristic, and unifying forces were preserved in all essential manifestations during the seventeenth and eighteenth centuries: in the *commedia dell'arte* (which kept a close link with its carnival origin), in Molière's comedies (related to the

---

[10] See J.B.L. du Tilliot, *Mémoires pour servir à l'histoire de la Fête des Foux, qui se faisoit autrefois dans plusieurs églises* (Lausanne, 1741); for example: 'Les Statuts Synodaux de l'Eglise de Lyon en 1566 et 1577 défendent avec beaucoup de rigueur les insolences de la Fête des Foux. Voici comment ils parlent: "Es jours de Fête des Innocens et autres, l'on ne doit souffrir es Eglises joüer jeux, Tragédies, farces, et exhiber spectacles ridicules avec masques, armes et tambourins, et autres choses indécentes qui se font en icelles, sous peine d'excommunication [...] Défendront les Curés, disent-ils ailleurs, sur peine d'excommunication, de mener danses, faire Bacchanales et autres insolences es Eglises ou es Cimetieres"' (Du Tilliot, pp. 36-7).

[11] See N. Temple, 'The Decline of Urban Festivities in Seventeenth-Century France', *Newsletter of the Society of Seventeenth-Century French Studies*, 3 (1981), pp. 79-86.

[12] See J. Heers, *Fêtes des fous et Carnavals* (Paris, 1983), pp. 298-9: 'La fête joyeuse des fous, sorte de cavalcade sans trame précise, assez débridée, finit, à n'en pas douter, par s'effacer devant le succès des divertissements beaucoup mieux ordonnés, davantage «pensés», du Carnaval. Celui-ci, pris en main dès l'origine par quelques groupes sociaux de la cité, finit, à la limite, par administrer des leçons de sagesse professionnelle et politique [...]. Fête davantage laïque, le Carnaval se trouve souvent marqué, altéré, par une volonté de gouverner la ville à travers la fête, par une teinte aristocratique souvent bien affichée et dans le choix des thèmes de la représentation, par le reflet d'une culture bien plus élitiste, courtoise, princière, humaniste'.

[13] M. Bakhtin, *Problems of Dostoevsky's Poetics*, ed. and trans. C. Emerson (Manchester, 1984), p. 130. D. Stanton comments on the ambivalent nature of carnival in seventeenth-century France in 'On *la contestation* and *le carnaval*: a paradoxical preface', *Actes de Banff: 1986*, ed. M. Bareau and others (Tübingen, 1987), pp. 123-41.

[14] *Dostoevsky*, p. 122

commedia dell'arte), in the comic novel and travesty of the seventeenth century
[...].[15]

The influence of *commedia dell'arte*, if not as obvious in *Les Amants magnifiques* as in some of Molière's other comedies, is manifest in the impertinent jester figure of Clitidas (played by Molière). Many of his scenes have the distinctive flavour of *commedia*: in Act I, scene iv, for example, there are echoes of a *lazzo* as Clitidas shuttles to and fro between the two rival princes, treacherously promising equal help to each; and another well-tried routine occurs in Act V, scene i, when Clitidas teases the melancholy Ériphile by delaying the news which she is longing to hear. Clitidas is a descendant of Harlequin, as he is also an ancestor of Marivaux's Arlequin and of Figaro.

Although the Court audience at Saint-Germain-en-Laye was about as far removed as could be imagined from the carnival's original audience in the public square or street,[16] *Les Amants magnifiques* nonetheless embodies the spirit of carnival in the way it obliterates the distinctions between performer and spectator. Bakhtin speaks of carnival as 'a pageant without footlights and without a division into performers and spectators. In carnival everyone is an active participant, everyone communes in the carnival act'.[17] *Les Amants magnifiques*, in the tradition of the great *ballets de cour*, provides the roles of Neptune and Apollon for the King, as well as dancing roles for certain courtiers, who all become participants, performing moreover with the author of the text.[18] (They appear in the same work, but not of course together in the same scenes: court carnival has its limits.)

Audience participation is only one aspect of the work's intrinsic theatricality, a theme placed to the fore from the first sentence of the 'Avant-Propos':

> Le Roi, qui ne veut que des choses extraordinaires dans tout ce qu'il entreprend, s'est proposé de donner à sa cour un divertissement qui fût composé de tous ceux que le théâtre peut fournir [...].

---

[15] M. Bakhtin, *Rabelais and His World*, trans. H. Iswolsky (Bloomington, 1984), p. 34. Compare p. 116, where Bakhtin speaks of a 'popular-festive tradition', surviving particularly in Molière.

[16] See *Dostoevsky*, p. 128.

[17] *Dostoevsky*, p. 122.

[18] The King did not dance the roles of Neptune and Apollon after the first performance, and some have doubted whether he danced them even on that occasion; however the *livre* printed for distribution at the first performance makes clear that the roles are intended for him: see *Œuvres de Molière*, ed. Despois and Mesnard, VII, pp. 354-5; and Beaussant, *Lully*, pp. 377-9. On the King's prowess as a performer, and on the reasons for his abandoning the stage in 1670, see R. Astier, 'Louis XIV, "premier danseur"', in *Sun King: the ascendancy of French culture during the reign of Louis XIV*, ed. D.L. Rubin (Washington, 1992), pp. 73-102.

The first scene is a spectacle which we discover, but only subsequently, to be a *performance* staged by Iphicrate to seduce Ériphile. Different types of spectacle follow, and an unusual feature of the structure is that the most elaborate musical section comes neither at the beginning, nor at the end, but in the middle of the work, between the second and third Acts. The *Troisième intermède*, in the form of a pastoral, is an ambitious piece of music, nothing less than a miniature opera in five scenes, whose structure (alternating scenes of ballet and pastoral sandwiched between a prologue and a finale) is a microcosm of the work as a whole.

The theme of the *Troisième intermède* likewise mirrors that of the larger work: three men in pursuit of one woman, who secretly loves one of the three. When the pastoral lovers seal their union by becoming spectators of a pastoral *dépit amoureux*, the effect of *mise en abyme* becomes dizzying. The King presents (and performs in) a spectacle for the Court, in which Timoclès presents a pastoral for the cold Ériphile, in which Tircis complains of the coldness of Caliste, and this pair, once they are reconciled, become spectators of a scene in which another pastoral pair quarrel and make up. When the actors join together at the end of the *intermède* to sing 'Amants, que vos querelles / Sont aimables et belles!', their words resonate in three different frames simultaneously.

Critical discussion of *Les Amants magnifiques* (and there has been little) has often focused on the complexity of theatrical illusion in the work: 'C'est la plus parfaitement télescopique des «mises en abyme» que le théâtre baroque [...] ait construites: le «théâtre sur le théâtre» deux fois dédoublé'.[19] But this is not a baroque effect comparable to, for example, the play of illusion in *L'Illusion comique*, where the spectators are teasingly confused as to the reality of what they see. In *Les Amants magnifiques*, Molière ensures that his audience remains fully aware of the frames which successively encapsulate the action, and there is a hint of parody in his exploitation of the play-within-a-play device; the King's megalomaniac desire for all-encompassing spectacle is a source of humour for the spectator—and of anxiety for Aristione:

> On enchaîne pour nous ici tant de divertissements les uns aux autres, que toutes nos heures sont retenues, et nous n'avons aucun moment à perdre, si nous voulons les goûter tous. (II, v)

---

[19] Beaussant, *Lully*, p. 376; see also L.E. Auld, 'Theatrical Illusion as Theme in *Les Amants magnifiques*', *Romance Notes*, 16 (1974), pp. 144-55; and J.D. Hubert, 'Theoretical Aspects of Fête and Theatricality in Seventeenth-Century France', in *Sun King*, pp. 35-44.

The sole occasion on which we become the unwitting victims of
theatrical illusion is in Act IV, scene ii, when Vénus appears before
Aristione and Ériphile; and whatever our suspicions about this *dea ex
machina* (and they depend very much on how the scene is produced), the
illusion is brutally punctured by Anaxarque at the start of the next
scene:

> Le stratagème a réussi. Notre Vénus a fait des merveilles; et l'admirable
> ingénieur qui s'est employé à cet artifice a si bien disposé tout, a coupé avec tant
> d'adresse le plancher de cette grotte, si bien caché ses fils de fer et tous ses
> ressorts, si bien ajusté ses lumières et habillé ses personnages, qu'il y a peu de
> gens qui n'y eussent été trompés. (IV, iii)

The carnivalesque is a potent means of breaking illusion and of
achieving defamiliarisation within a comic framework, and it functions
in this episode to great effect.[20] Far from celebrating baroque theatrical
illusion, Molière celebrates its subversion.

The carnivalesque nature of *Les Amants magnifiques* is evident, too,
in the hybrid nature of its genre. The *comédie-ballet* was a new genre,
as Molière had acknowledged in the 'avertissement' to *Les Fâcheux*
('c'est un mélange qui est nouveau pour nos théâtres'), and more than
that, it was an intrinsically unstable one.[21] Each of Molière's essays in
the form represents a different solution to the challenge of combining
actors and dancers, speech and music, and *Les Amants magnifiques*,
described on the title-page as a 'comédie mêlée de musique et d'entrées
de ballet', marks one of his most ambitious attempts to date. It is
significant that Molière replaces Benserade as the author of the *vers de
cour*, so that, for the first time in a *comédie-ballet*, he is in sole charge
of the whole text. If in retrospect the work can be seen as the last great
ballet de cour (and no later work for the Court would include a role for
the King), it is also one in which Lully, with Molière's help, is feeling
his way towards an aesthetic of French opera. In the central (and
dominant) pastoral episode, Lully abandons the traditional *airs de cour*
and moves towards a style of recitative which within a couple of years
would become the hallmark of the *tragédie lyrique*; the trio sung by the
three *bergers* in scene iv ('Dormez, dormez, beaux yeux') is of
particular beauty, and entirely operatic in its musical form.[22]

---

[20] Compare: 'Carnival [...] is a *means for displaying otherness*: carnival makes familiar relations
strange' (M. Holquist, *Dialogism: Bakhtin and his world* (London, 1990), p. 89).

[21] See A. Coe, '*Ballet en comédie* or *comédie en ballet*? *La Princesse d'Élide* and *Les Amants
magnifiques*', *Cahiers du Dix-septième: an interdisciplinary journal*, 2 (1988), pp. 109-21.

[22] See Beaussant, *Lully*, pp. 371-5.

Les Amants magnifiques is a work of generic experimentation, standing at the culmination of one tradition and on the threshold of another. Parody is a defining element in the carnivalesque structure of such a work: 'To the pure genres (epic, tragedy)', writes Bakhtin, 'parody is organically alien; to the carnivalized genres it is, on the contrary, organically inherent'.[23] There is an obvious pastiche of the poet whom Molière had displaced, Benserade, in the verses declaimed by Neptune at the end of the first *intermède* (so successful a pastiche that some in the audience assumed that Benserade himself must be the author of the verses—surely the response which Molière was hoping for). The situation in Act III, scene i, when the two rival princes find themselves obliged to pay court to a mere general, imitates Corneille's *Don Sanche d'Aragon* (I, iii), and in doing so misleads the audience into anticipating a recognition scene in which Sostrate, like Don Sanche, will turn out to be of noble birth. The audience is doubly teased, and the parody all the greater, because the recognition which we are expecting had by Molière's time become distinctly unfashionable.[24] The *dépit amoureux* in the third *intermède* is freely adapted from Horace's famous ode 'Donec gratus eram tibi', reinforcing the effect of *mise en abyme* in that pivotal scene. And when Sostrate in the first scene exclaims 'Ah! mon cœur, ah! mon cœur, où m'avez-vous jeté?', there is an unmistakable allusion to Molière's own earlier pastoral, *Mélicerte*. Nor are parody and allusion confined to language alone: Lully looks back to his operatic forebears (and reveals his operatic ambitions) in the exquisite trio 'Dormez, dormez, beaux yeux', which is calqued on the chorus 'Dormite, begl'occhi, dormite', in Act II, scene ix of Luigi Rossi's *Orfeo* (performed at the Palais-Royal in 1647), one of the first operas seen in Paris.

The carnivalesque spirit is evident also in the linguistic dialogism of the work. There is constant play with linguistic register as the conventional language of love is relativised by such phrases as 'du pied au cul' (I, ii) and 'un beau petit morveux de prince' (I, iv). In the scenes shared between Clitidas and Sostrate, Clitidas repeatedly brings down to earth the poetic rhythms of Sostrate's *précieux* prose:

> SOSTRATE: Ah! Clitidas, je tremble avec raison, et tous les Gaulois du monde ensemble sont bien moins redoutables que deux beaux yeux pleins de charmes.

---

[23] *Dostoevsky*, p. 127

[24] See T. Cave, *Recognitions: a study in poetics* (Oxford, 1988), pp. 84-5.

> CLITIDAS: Je ne suis pas de cet avis, et je sais bien pour moi qu'un seul Gaulois, l'épée à la main, me feroit beaucoup plus trembler que cinquante beaux yeux ensemble les plus charmants du monde. (I, i)[25]

This exchange exemplifies a recurrent motif: the discussion of rhetoric and its efficacy. Clitidas, for example, creates comedy by discussing rhetoric as a substitute for using it:

> Je devrois vous faire peut-être, pour orner mon récit, une description étendue du sanglier dont je parle, mais vous vous en passerez, s'il vous plaît, et je me contenterai de vous dire que c'étoit un fort vilain animal. (V, i)

The scenes between Aristione and the two rival princes make the same point, though more subtly. In lauding repeatedly the spectacles mounted by the princes, Aristione resorts to hyperbole so extravagant as to be meaningless (the effect is similar to that of the rhetoric in the opening pages of *La Princesse de Clèves*):

> Cette fête [...] vient de produire à nos yeux quelque chose de si noble, de si grand et de si majestueux, que le Ciel même ne sauroit aller au delà, et je puis dire assurément qu'il n'y a rien dans l'univers qui s'y puisse égaler. (I, ii)

Verbal contests and 'exchanges of gifts' are examples of what Bakhtin calls the 'accessory rituals of carnival', and he speaks of 'abundance as an aspect of carnivalistic utopia'.[26] As the princes seek to overwhelm through the artifice of elaborate spectacle, so Aristione responds in kind by overwhelming them with the artifice of elaborate language; in neither case is the artifice persuasive, though in both cases the contemplation of the artifice is a source of considerable pleasure. Aristione herself affects immunity to commonplace rhetoric:

> De grâce, Prince, ôtons ces charmes et ces attraits: vous savez que ce sont des mots que je retranche des compliments qu'on me veut faire [...]. Prince, je ne donne point dans tous ces galimatias où donnent la plupart des femmes. (I, ii)

This rhetoric of non-rhetoric is, however, equally unpersuasive; and Aristione's hyperbole inevitably turns to self-parody as the most compelling mode of expression:

---

[25] Compare: 'Les plaintes et aveux de Sostrate, bien qu'écrits en prose, sont abondamment imprégnés de la rhétorique et des rythmes des genres héroïques et tragiques traditionnellement composés en vers. Octosyllabes, hémistiches tantôt isolés, tantôt essaimant en alexandrins non-rimés, y font écho aux vers et à la prose de *La Princesse d'Élide* et de *Mélicerte*. Par deux fois, l'intervention prosaïque de Clitidas interrompt la diction poétique, et du coup, la met particulièrement en relief' (Guicharnaud, 'Les trois niveaux critiques', pp. 32-3).

[26] *Dostoevsky*, p. 125.

> Les mêmes paroles toujours se présentent à dire, il faut toujours s'écrier: «Voilà qui est admirable, il ne se peut rien de plus beau, cela passe tout ce qu'on a jamais vu.» (III, i)

The carnivalisation of language generated by the self-conscious juxtaposition of contrasting linguistic registers is reinforced by the presence of alternative (and more effective) modes of expression. When Sostrate refuses to speak the name of the person he loves, Clitidas deciphers it in Sostrate's eyes (I, i). The second and fifth *intermèdes* introduce 'des pantomimes'; the word was not current, and Molière defines it for his audience: 'Ce sont des personnes qui, par leurs pas, leurs gestes et leurs mouvements, expriment aux yeux toutes choses, et on appelle cela Pantomimes' (I, v). In stark contrast to the princes' noisy and elaborate spectacles in the other *intermèdes*, the 'pantomimes' reflect sympathetically the feelings of the princess, and communicate them simply, but forcefully ('vos danseurs, qui expriment si bien toutes les passions', IV, v): mime and dance supersede language. Elsewhere in the work, as in all the *comédies-ballets*, language is repeatedly overtaken by music, and spoken prose combines with sung verse to produce a work which is truly polyphonic.

The interplay of dissonant linguistic registers is of course a fundamental comic device (and notably present in *commedia dell'arte*), but dialogism here runs much deeper, as language is relativised by both dance and music. The omnipresent theme of rhetorical display reduces language to the status of spectacle, a medium to be used with relish, but certainly not one which can accord us privileged access to truth. The notion that there is only one right way of expressing an idea is fundamental to classical thinking about language: 'Entre toutes les différentes expressions qui peuvent rendre une seule de nos pensées,' writes La Bruyère, 'il n'y en a qu'une qui soit la bonne.'[27] *Les Amants magnifiques* confronts this monologism head-on, with a language of carnival in which rival discourses oppose each other in a state of constant dialogic tension. Simple truth can never be simply expressed, or indeed expressed at all (we need only think of the delightfully tantalizing love-making between Ériphile and Sostrate). More elaborate attempts at persuasive and imposing spectacle prove to be equally unviable (Ériphile is unmoved by the princes' extravagant shows of

---

[27] *Les Caractères*, ed. R. Garapon (Paris, 1962), p. 71. See also my article 'The Singular Voice: monologism and French classical discourse', *Continuum*, 1 (1989), pp. 175-202.

affection). We are entertained by the spectacle of language, but at the cost of being taught to mistrust it.[28]

Bakhtin speaks of 'carnivalistic laughter' as 'directed toward something higher—toward a shift of authorities and truths, a shift of world orders.'[29] At the level of plot this is seen in *Les Amants magnifiques* in the jester and astrologer figures, both of whom were allegedly added by Molière to the plot outline suggested by the King. In creating for himself the role of Clitidas, the jester or *plaisant de cour*, Molière invokes a quintessential figure of carnival. This character, quite apart from its connections with *commedia*, has wide literary resonance, and the *fou* or *sot* has a long pedigree in carnivalesque literature of the fifteenth and sixteenth centuries, notably in the satirical genre of the *sottie*.[30] Clitidas plays the fool from the first scene of Act One, when he smells love in the air and reads a name in another man's eyes; yet there is a serious side to the fooling:

> The character of the *fou* [...] is seen as lacking in common sense, yet he is also a truth-speaker. The *sot* is a striking example of the medieval fool's freedom to criticize [...]. Yet there is nothing stern or humorless about the fool's truth-telling. On the contrary, he lets fall the most outrageous criticisms in a spirit of *gaieté*. The *sots* never tire of rejoicing.[31]

Clitidas is much indebted to this late medieval stereotype and, while teasing and chiding Sostrate, he also boasts of his privilege of speaking back-to-front:

> Vous savez que je suis auprès de [la jeune princesse] en quelque espèce de faveur, que j'y ai les accès ouverts, et qu'à force de me tourmenter, je me suis acquis le privilége de me mêler à la conversation et parler à tort et à travers de toutes choses. Quelquefois cela ne me réussit pas, mais quelquefois aussi cela me réussit. (I, i)

In the hands of the fool, the language of carnival deflates all monologic assertion; and Anaxarque, in attempting to remain aloof from this comic liberty of speech, makes himself foolish:

> Il y a une chose qui est fâcheuse dans votre cour, que tout le monde y prenne liberté de parler, et que le plus honnête homme y soit exposé aux railleries du premier méchant plaisant. (I, ii)

---

[28] In the 'Préface' to *Tartuffe*, Molière describes a theory of language at the opposite extreme to the carnivalesque: 'Puisqu'on doit discourir des choses et non pas des mots, et que la plupart des contrariétés viennent de ne se pas entendre et d'envelopper dans un même mot des choses opposées, il ne faut qu'ôter le voile de l'équivoque et regarder ce qu'est la comédie en soi, pour voir si elle est condamnable'. This response to his critics is clearly tactical—and possibly ironic?

[29] *Dostoevsky*, p. 127.

[30] See *Rabelais*, pp. 5, 15.

[31] H. Arden, *Fools' Plays: a study of satire in the 'sottie'* (Cambridge, 1980), p. 161.

The carnivalesque character of the role of Clitidas (played in 1954 at the Comédie Française by Robert Hirsch) was well brought out in the 1988 production by the acting of Alan Boone, whose virtuoso comic agility, both physical and linguistic, brought to the part of the *plaisant de cour* something of the Shakespearean clown. To describe Clitidas as a 'relatively "straight" role' which 'helps to assert the primacy of reason, common sense and the natural order of things' is surely misguided,[32] and not only because it ignores the lessons of performance: it also leaves out of account the pivotal role of carnival. If we are looking for a *raisonneur* figure, Sostrate comes closest in the long speech in which he mocks belief in astrology;[33] but even here we must exercise caution: it is never easy to preach reason in the context of carnival.

Clitidas is not Molière's first *plaisant de cour* (there had been Moron, in *La Princesse d'Élide*), but his character has an unprecedented astringency arising from his antagonistic relationship with Anaxarque:

> Le métier de plaisant n'est pas comme celui d'astrologue. Bien mentir et bien plaisanter sont deux choses fort différentes, et il est bien plus facile de tromper les gens que de les faire rire. (I, ii)

Nowhere else in Molière do we find this powerful juxtaposition of fool and astrologer, though there is an analogue in earlier carnivalesque literature, in the *Sottie nouvelle de l'astrologue* (1498). The play consists of a dialogue between three *sots* and an astrologer, and from remarks made in the work it is clear that it is one of a series of *sotties* in which the same astrologer figure appears alongside the fools.[34] The satirical targets of the play are political and not astrological, so that the fool and astrologer figures are not opposed as in *Les Amants magnifiques*; even so, the overlap in the dramatis personae of the two works anchors them in the same carnivalesque tradition.

Molière's astrologer thus owes nothing to the farcical astrologers of d'Ouville's *Jodelet Astrologue* (1645) and of Thomas Corneille's *Le Feint Astrologue* (1650), both descended from Calderón's *El Astrólogo fingido*; Anaxarque is a sinister figure (his name means 'he who commands kings') whose hold over the princess Aristione resembles that of Tartuffe over Orgon—except that Aristione is never disabused of her

---

[32] W. D. Howarth, *Molière: a playwright and his audience* (Cambridge, 1982), p. 220.

[33] 'Transformer tout en or, faire vivre éternellement, guérir par des paroles, se faire aimer de qui l'on veut, savoir tous les secrets de l'avenir [...]: tout cela est charmant, sans doute; et il y a des gens qui n'ont aucune peine à en comprendre la possibilité: cela leur est le plus aisé du monde à concevoir. Mais pour moi, je vous avoue que mon esprit grossier a quelque peine à le comprendre et à le croire, et j'ai toujours trouvé cela trop beau pour être véritable' (III, i).

[34] See *Recueil général des sotties*, ed. E. Picot, 3 vols (Paris, 1902-12), I , p. 199.

error. The character of Anaxarque is said to be partly based on Jean-Baptiste Morin (1583-1656), an astrologer who had engaged in a bitter polemic with Gassendi and who was vilified by Bayle.[35] But Molière's attack on astrology was not limited to one individual. In choosing this as his target, he was tackling a subject as topically sensitive as medicine or religion, and one which similarly touched on questions of authority and authoritarianism.

Discussion of astrology was expressly forbidden in the statutes of the Académie des Sciences, founded in 1666, and in a sermon on February 2nd of the same year ('Soumission aux volontés de Dieu'), referring to the recent appearance of a comet, Bossuet attacks 'astrologues' and 'faiseurs de pronostics'. La Fontaine's fable 'L'Astrologue qui se laisse tomber dans un puits' (II, 13), dating from 1668, is savage:

> Charlatans, faiseurs d'horoscope,
> Quittez les cours des princes de l'Europe.

La Fontaine returned to the attack (1678-1679) in 'L'Horoscope' (VIII, 16), and in 1682 there was a royal edict on the subject.[36] The most prominent satirical treatment of astrology and related questions is to be found in a work exactly contemporary with *Les Amants magnifiques*, the abbé de Villars's *Le Comte de Gabalis ou Entretiens sur les sciences secrètes* (1670). Villars pours scorn on simple belief in such things as oracles, and, like Molière, thereby runs the risk of criticism from the Church. In the 'Lettre à Monseigneur', the postface to *Le Comte de Gabalis*, he forestalls the argument in a way which recalls Molière's defences of *Tartuffe*:

> Comme toutes [les erreurs de la Cabale] sont sur les choses Divines, outre la difficulté qu'il y a de faire rire un honneste homme sur quelque sujet que ce soit: il est de plus tres dangereux de railler en celuy-cy, & il est fort à craindre que la devotion ne semble y estre interessée.[37]

Using irony to defend his use of irony, Villars responds in the third person to the hypothetical criticism that it is inappropriate to adopt 'ce tour plaisant' in attacking such a serious target. He explains the mechanism by which humour subverts orthodoxy in what amounts to a description of carnivalesque laughter:

---

[35] See Molière, *Œuvres complètes*, ed. G. Couton, 2 vols, Pléiade (Paris, 1971), II, pp. 643-4; and *Œuvres de Molière*, ed. Despois and Mesnard, VII, pp. 369-72.

[36] See La Fontaine, *Œuvres complètes*, ed. R. Groos and J. Schiffrin, Pléiade, I (Paris, 1954), p. 686, note 1.

[37] Montfaucon de Villars, 'Lettre à Monseigneur', *Le Comte de Gabalis*, ed. R. Laufer (Paris, 1963), p. 140.

> Mon Amy répond à cela [...] qu'ayant voulu d'abord essayer sur ce sujet le
> style Dogmatique, il s'estoit trouvé si ridicule luy-mesme de traiter serieusement
> des sottises, qu'il avoit jugé plus à propos de tourner ce ridicule contre le
> Seigneur Comte de Gabalis. La Cabale (dit-il) est du nombre de ces chimeres,
> qu'on authorise quand on les combat gravement, & qu'on ne doit entreprendre
> de détruire qu'en se joüant.[38]

Villars's words might equally well have been used by Molière to describe the function of carnival in *Les Amants magnifiques*.

The 'Avant-propos' of *Les Amants magnifiques* claims that the plot was suggested by the King (who, by implication, is accused of plagiarising Corneille): 'Sa Majesté a choisi pour sujet deux princes rivaux, qui [...] régalent à l'envi une jeune princesse et sa mère de toutes les galanteries dont ils se peuvent aviser.' (This was not the King's first attempt at literary collaboration: he had previously suggested that a character be added to *Les Fâcheux* and had chosen from Tasso the theme for *Les Plaisirs de l'Ile enchantée*; he would later choose the theme for Quinault's *Amadis*.)[39] The King thus commissioned and shaped a work which begins and ends with his own perfomances: it is a bold celebration of royal authorship as well as of royal authority.

Yet the work also celebrates the subversion of that authority.[40] The presence of carnival undermines the dogmatic assertions of Anaxarque, indeed all authoritarian or monologic assertion, including ultimately the King's grandiose ambitions for the work itself. Hence the dialogic tensions which characterise this piece, and which reveal a structure not so much disjointed as multi-levelled. The function of the carnivalesque, says Bakhtin, is to offer 'the chance to have a new outlook on the world, to realize the relative nature of all that exists, and to enter a completely new order of things.'[41] It is in this joyous spirit of liberation that the unity of this *comédie-ballet* resides. 'Le moyen de contester ce qui est moulé?', asks Molière / Clitidas (III, i). An answer is suggested by the very form of *Les Amants magnifiques*, by the manner in which it challenges our assumptions and expectations. As Aristione says, 'des bagatelles comme celles-là peuvent occuper agréablement les plus sérieuses personnes' (III, i). Or, as Béralde will remark in a later play: 'Le carnaval autorise cela'.

---

[38] Ibid.

[39] See P. Burke, *The Fabrication of Louis XIV* (New Haven, 1992), p. 69.

[40] Using the sociological evidence of courtly gift exchanges, A.E. Zanger reaches a parallel conclusion: 'The Spectacular Gift: rewriting the royal scenario in Molière's *Les Amants magnifiques*', *Romanic Review*, 81 (1990), pp. 173-88

[41] *Rabelais*, p. 34.

The Role of the Past in Racine's
Andromaque

BY

CHRISTINE MCGARRY

UNIVERSITY OF GLASGOW

> The Past is not separate and completed but an ever-developing part of a
> changing present.[1]

Our past will always be a part of our present. Our recollections of
different elements of the past, whether periods spanning several years
or brief moments, influence our feelings, decisions and actions as we
confront new situations. The dramatist, with a few hours at his or her
disposal, is faced with the problem of acquainting the audience with
elements from the life experience of the characters on stage which may
account for their present actions, or explain why present decisions
should be so difficult, thus providing scope for dramatic conflict or
suspense. Gouhier explains the relationship between the spectator and
the past lives of the characters on stage:

> Croire que Hamlet existe, c'est croire qu'existe aussi ou qu'ont existé tous ceux
> qui habitent la mémoire de Hamlet, de sorte que mon jugement déploie un
> immense passé dans la profondeur temporelle de l'action comme il projette un
> immense espace autour de la petite zone découpée par le jeu.[2]

It is the purpose of this article to explore certain aspects of the
relationship of the past with the action on stage, and to examine the
extent to which the characters have control over their own memories
and those of others.

The dramatist must make the past become present on stage. In the
case of *Andromaque*, while the seventeenth-century audience would no
doubt be familiar with the main events of the Trojan war, thus, one
might assume, facilitating Racine's task, it is worth remembering that,
from a dramatic point of view, the objective 'reality' of the war is
largely irrelevant. The only thing that matters in terms of dramatic

---

[1] A. Mendilow, *The Position of the Present in Fiction*, in *The Theory of the Novel*, ed. P. Stevick
(New York, London, 1967), p. 270.

[2] *Le Théâtre et l'existence* (Paris, 1952), p. 29.

impact on the spectator is the particular memory each individual character has of his or her past. This notion also applies in real life, as is explained by Mead:

> It is idle, at least for the purposes of experience, to have recourse to a 'real' past within which we are making constant discoveries; for that past must be set over against a present within which the emergent appears, and the past, which must then be looked at from the standpoint of the emergent, becomes a different past.[3]

Critical approaches to the play this century have justifiably emphasised the important role of the past and have devoted particular attention to evocations of Troy.[4] Critics seem to be in general agreement that the motivations and actions of Pyrrhus and Andromaque are largely determined by the events of the war and the different perception which each has of them. The past lives on not merely in the present recollections the characters have of it, but also in the way in which characters are seen to be a continuation of genealogical lines. Each character is inextricably linked with his or her ancestral past,[5] a past whose fatality, as Poulet infers, weighs heavily on the present action:

> ... the whole Racinian drama is presented as the intrusion of a fatal past, of a determining past, of a past of efficient cause, into a present that seeks desperately to become independent of it. (p.76)

Some studies have gone so far as to see the play as a re-enactment of the Trojan war, with Hector once again playing the leading role.[6] His presence, either in Andromaque herself:

> S'il me perd, je consens qu'il me retrouve en toi. (1024)[7]

or most significantly in the shape of her son Astyanax:

---

[3] *The Philosophy of the Present* (Chicago, London, 1932), p. 2.

[4] For example, see J. Le Hir, 'Puissance et prestige du passé dans *Andromaque* de Racine' in *Études classiques*, 33, no. 4 (1965), 401-11; J. Vier, 'A propos d'*Andromaque*: réflexions sur Hector', *L'École*, 45 (17 oct 1950), 65-67; R. Barthes, *Sur Racine* (Paris, 1960), pp. 78-86; and, especially, G. Poulet's 'Notes on Racinian Time', in *Racine: Modern Judgements*, ed. R.C. Knight (London, 1969), pp. 75-87.

[5] See H.T. Barnwell, 'Racine's *Andromaque*: new myth for old' in *Myth and its Making in the French Theatre: Studies presented to W.D. Howarth*, ed. M.J. Freeman et al. (Cambridge, 1988), 53-70 (p. 61).

[6] J. D. Hubert , *Essai d'exégèse racinienne* (Paris, 1956), who also stresses the moral superiority of Hector and Andromaque over Pyrrhus and the Greeks, and J. Vier, art. cit. See also J. O'Brien, 'Characterizing the Past: Racine's *Andromaque*' in *Racine: Appraisal and Reappraisal*, ed. E. Forman (Bristol, 1991), pp. 38-53 (p. 42).

[7] Quotations from Racine are taken from *Œuvres*, ed. P. Mesnard, 8 vols (Paris, 1865-73).

'C'est Hector, disait-elle en l'embrassant toujours,
Voilà ses yeux, sa bouche, et déjà son audace;
C'est lui-même, cher époux, que j'embrasse.' (652-4)[8]

ensures that on this metaphorical battlefield of human emotions it is the
Trojans who emerge victorious. Pyrrhus, Oreste and Hermione are
made to pay, in terms of the suffering of unrequited love, for the Greek
exploits on the literal battlefield of Troy. Markedly less abundant are
detailed discussions of the linguistic means through which the past is
evoked,[9] and the essential relationship such evocations have with the
structure of the plot.[10] It is therefore these particular aspects which will
be the focus of this study.

When we think of the role of the past in *Andromaque*, we may recall
without much difficulty the highly emotive and hauntingly poetic
evocation of the 'nuit éternelle' by Andromaque in Act III, scene viii,
and juxtapose it with Pyrrhus' dismissive, not to say insensitive,
confession—'J'ai fait des malheureux, sans doute' (313)—highlighting
the gulf which their respective perceptions of the war places between
them. However, it is not always appreciated to what extent references to
the past permeate the play in much less obvious ways, and the variety of
functions which such references perform. While this article does not
claim to be an exhaustive study of this vast area, some of the least
explored aspects of the use of past time will be examined in a fresh
light.

The use of Troy for strategic purposes has already been suggested by
Verhoeff,[11] who quotes the single example of Oreste's first dialogue
with Pyrrhus, where a request is made in such a way as to solicit a
refusal:

Dans les confrontations qui opposent les personnages, Troie est invoquée pour
des besoins stratégiques, comme prétexte, pour parvenir à d'autres buts ou pour
accabler et réfuter l'adversaire.

---

[8] R. Kuhn goes furthest in assigning to Astyanax a purely symbolic role, 'The Palace of Broken
Words: Reflexions on Racine's Andromaque', *Romanic Review*, 70 (1979), 336-45 (pp. 337-8).

[9] J.B. Ratermanis, *Les Formes verbales dans les tragédies de Racine* (Paris, 1972), uses an
examination of verbal forms to demonstrate the extent of attachment to the past in *Andromaque*. J. C.
Lapp, *Aspects of Racinian Tragedy* (Toronto, 1955), pp. 38-55 deals more generally with specific
references to precise periods of pre-dramatic time.

[10] See Barnwell, op. cit., and H. Verhoeff, 'Troie, thème et structure dans *Andromaque*', in *Re-
lectures raciniennes: nouvelles approches du discours tragique*, ed. R.L. Barnett (Paris, Seattle,
Tübingen, 1986), 229-51.

[11] Art. cit., p. 235.

Oreste follows Pylade's advice to: 'Pressez, demandez tout, pour ne rien obtenir' (140). If we look at this scene in more detail, however, we can see the extent to which references to the past form an essential part of Oreste's strategy to manipulate Pyrrhus. The first step in Oreste's engineering of Pyrrhus's reaction involves a reminder of his illustrious past and his famous father:

> Oui, comme ses exploits nous admirons vos coups:
> Hector tomba sous lui, Troie expira sous vous;
> Et vous avez montré, par une heureuse audace,
> Que le fils seul d'Achille a pu remplir sa place. (147-50)

This deliberate swelling of Pyrrhus's already inflated ego ensures that the reproach subsequently delivered, like that to a naughty child who has done something silly, is met with stern indignation: 'Ne vous souvient-il plus, Seigneur, quel fut Hector?' (155). The implication in this line is of some kind of incapacity on the part of Pyrrhus to recognise an obvious danger. This, and the suggestion that Pyrrhus should *fear* the son of Hector, understandably come as an insult to the experienced warrior who has just been reminded of his own military prowess as well as of that of his father. He is therefore bound to refuse to bow his head and meekly hand back something he has no right to possess. The strategy works, but we note that Pyrrhus then uses the same strategic device of referring to the past, and in particular the ancestral past, to slight Oreste.

> Qui croiroit en effet qu'une telle entreprise
> Du fils d'Agamemnon méritât l'entremise;
> Qu'un peuple tout entier, tant de fois triomphant,
> N'eût daigné conspirer que la mort d'un enfant? (177-80)

As Barnwell points out,[12] Pyrrhus evokes strikingly different memories of the past to reinforce his argument:

> Je ne vois que des tours que la cendre a couvertes,
> Un fleuve teint de sang, des campagnes desertes,
> Un enfant dans les fers [...] (201-3)

Pyrrhus and Oreste each select, from their respective reservoir of memories, the images best suited to the arguments they presently wish to make. Similarly, they are playing with two views of Astyanax. In the present he is a child, and as such fears concerning him seem ridiculous. This is the view Pyrrhus takes in Act I, scene ii. For Oreste, the threat

---

[12] Art. cit., p. 62.

posed by the child can be seen to stem also from the past. The fears he
expresses concerning the expectation of what the son may become in the
future are based on the past experience of the father. That these views
are not in fact held with any great conviction, but are rather determined
by what will best suit present purposes, is shown a few lines later. In his
conversation with Andromaque, attempting to bribe her into
submission, Pyrrhus contradicts what he has just said to Oreste:[13] 'Votre
Ilion encor peut sortir de sa cendre' (330). In Act II, scene iv, Pyrrhus
quotes loyalty to the Greeks and to the memory of his father as his
reason for deciding to surrender Astyanax to the Greek ambassador,
once again in direct contradiction to his earlier views: 'J'ai songé,
comme vous, qu'à la Grèce, à mon père [...]' (609). This *coup de théâtre*
occurs at a crucial point in the plot. Oreste has been charged with giving
Pyrrhus an ultimatum, and in a monologue he has just expressed his
confidence that Pyrrhus will not release Astyanax, in which case
Hermione has promised to marry him. The shock therefore prompts a
similar reversal on his part, as he suddenly takes up Pyrrhus's earlier
position: 'C'est acheter la paix du sang d'un malheureux' (616).

The extent of such strategic uses of the past can be explored still
further. If we return to Act I, we see that the initial pretext for
Pyrrhus's refusal to release Astyanax is in fact the time element. It
would, he asserts, have been acceptable to kill the child at the time of
the war: 'Tout était juste alors [...]' (209). Loyalty to the past is used, as
we have seen, as a pretext for Pyrrhus to hand over Astyanax. The real
reason for his desire to protect the child is of course his interest in the
mother. Proof of the lack of any real conviction in his 'all-is-fair-in-
love-and-war' attitude, expressed in his indignant 'Mais que ma cruauté
survive à ma colère?' (214), is not hard to find. Unable to accept with
good grace Andromaque's refusal to return his love, his thwarted
passion and jealousy do indeed lead him to new cruelties. His brutality
cannot be relegated to the past, as he would wish, but continues to
manifest itself in the face of fresh provocations.

> Je n'épargnerai rien dans ma juste colère [...] (369)

> Je ne condamne plus un courroux légitime [...] (613)

Ironically, though he may be able to use the past to suit his own ends,
the past itself has in turn a power to influence him which is far beyond

---

[13] Ibid. p. 64. See also P. Allen, 'The Role of Myth in Racine: *Andromaque, Iphigénie, Phèdre'*,
in *Myth and Legend in French Literature. Essays in honour of A.J. Steele*, ed. K. Aspley, D. Bellos
and P. Sharratt (London, 1982), 93-116 (p. 101).

his control. The role of the past in the true motive for his change of heart is revealed in his conversation with Phoenix in the following scene (Act II, scene v). Since his last meeting with his confidant he has witnessed an off-stage encounter between Andromaque and her son: 'Cent fois le nom d'Hector est sorti de sa bouche' (650). Pyrrhus desperately wants Andromaque to forget the past, to forget his own part in the massacre of her family, and most especially to forget Hector. He does not see Astyanax as being synonymous with Hector because he wants to deny that Hector can live on, especially as he appears to do so in the memory of the woman he loves. This explains the strength of his reaction to hearing these words spoken by Andromaque. He cannot control his jealousy. Frustration at Andromaque's inability to forget Hector will cause him to direct his anger at a child who is a constant reminder to his mother of her love for the dead Trojan hero. If Hector lives on in the child, the child must be destroyed. It is the tender kiss which Andromaque gives to 'l'image d'Hector' (1016) which provokes Pyrrhus's decision to hand over Astyanax to Oreste. His true feelings are revealed to Pylade in the following scene.

> Et quelle est sa pensée? Attend-elle en ce jour
> Que je lui laisse un fils pour nourrir son amour? (655-6)

Echoes of the past seem to mock Pyrrhus as he finds himself powerless to bury them. By destroying the last tangible reminder of Hector, he will certainly destroy any aspirations he may have of winning the love of Andromaque. While she may be his captive in a literal sense, he is a prisoner not only of his love for her but of the past itself.

A further source of irony is that even with his own words, he often inadvertently causes the past to work against him. When, in Act I, scene iv, he attempts to change Andromaque's attitude to the past to one similar to his own, the language he chooses and his inability to accept that she cannot or does not share his views, have serious dramatic consequences. His use of the words 'Ilion', 'cendre' and 'murs relevés' serve only to remind her of the gulf that separates her from Pyrrhus. Her reaction is one of disgust, contempt and an overwhelming desire to flee his presence. His attempt to compare his present sufferings with the ones he himself has caused: 'Je souffre tous les maux que j'ai faits devant Troie.' (318) results in a further distancing from the woman he is attempting to win over.

Andromaque, more than any other character, has a genuine attachment to the past, often against her own interests. Her evocation of

Troy in Act III, scene viii, leaves us in no doubt. She does not want to, much less feels she should, forget the past, even if the life of her son is at stake: 'Dois-je les oublier, s'il ne s'en souvient plus?' (992) However, as Barnwell points out,[14] even she uses her 'souvenir cruel' on other occasions as part of an argument. In Act I, scene iv, she tries to talk Pyrrhus into sparing her son without demanding anything from her in return.

> Malgré moi, s'il le faut, lui donner un asile:
> Seigneur, voilà des soins dignes du fils d'Achille. (309-10)

She casts aspersions upon the ancestry of her interlocutor, in the same way as did Pyrrhus and Oreste in scene ii of the same act, for manipulative purposes. In Act IV, scene iv, she again resorts to a similar tactic. In an attempt to persuade Hermione to plead her case with Pyrrhus, she reminds her of the way in which she prompted Hector to show kindness towards Hermione's mother.

> Hélas! lorsque lassés de dix ans de misère,
> Les Troyens en courroux menaçoient votre mère,
> J'ai su de mon Hector lui procurer l'appui
> Vous pouvez sur Pyrrhus ce que j'ai pu sur lui. (873-6)

This stratagem does not succeed with Hermione, whose bitterness and jealousy render such examples from the past ineffective, but this does not prevent Andromaque from using it again with Pyrrhus. In this encounter she wishes him to follow the example of his own ancestors.

> Jadis Priam soumis fut respecté d'Achille:
> J'attendais de son fils encor plus de bonté.
> Pardonne, cher Hector, à ma crédulité. (938-40)

Pyrrhus is largely untouched by this particular memory of the past. In reply to this entreaty by Andromaque, he reveals how much his idea of honourable behaviour towards captives differs from that of his father:

> Songez-y: je vous laisse; et je viendrai vous prendre
> Pour vous mener au temple ou ce fils doit m'attendre;
> Et là vous me verrez, soumis ou furieux,
> Vous couronner, Madame, ou le perdre à vos yeux. (973-6)

---

[14] Ibid. p. 64.

Andromaque's attempts at exploiting the strategic potential of references to the past are, then, futile. The irony is that it is her genuine attachment to the past which wields such destructive power over Pyrrhus.

Hermione is often seen as one of the most archaic figures in the play. Her views are shaped by fidelity to her father, her homeland and the legal ties which bind her to Pyrrhus.[15] Indeed, her main accusation against Pyrrhus seems to be his failure to keep his promise—'L'infidèle' (515). However, if we look at the text in more detail it becomes clear that her attachment to the past is not at all as deep-seated as may at first appear. It is she who perhaps more than any other character, manipulates the past to suit her own ends.

Pyrrhus has humiliated her, and in an attempt to persuade Oreste to avenge her she denies her love for Pyrrhus by ascribing her fidelity to the exigencies of filial duty:

> J'ai passé dans l'Epire, ou j'étois relégée:
> Mon père l'ordonnoit. Mais qui sait si depuis
> Je n'ai point en secret partagé vos ennuis? (522-4)

Her true feelings come through when Oreste suggests that Pyrrhus does not love her:

> Jugez-vous que ma vue inspire des mépris,
> Qu'elle allume en un cœur des feux si peu durables? (552-3)

She adheres to the idea that Pyrrhus' feelings cannot have died, because her own have not. She sees in the past only what she wants to see, Pyrrhus' promise but not Oreste's devotion. When Oreste, responding to Hermione's apparently more sympathetic approach to him, suggests that they should leave Épire together, Hermione again resorts to loyalty to the past, to State, to history and to old rivalries as a pretext for her to stay:

> Songez quelle honte pour nous
> Si d'une Phrygienne il devenait l'époux. (571-2)

In one final attempt she tries to use the power of the Greeks' hatred for the Trojans, rooted deeply in the past, to force Pyrrhus' hand.

> De la part de mon père allez lui faire entendre
> Que l'ennemi des Grecs ne peut être son gendre:
> Du Troyen ou de moi faites-le décider. (585-7)

---

[15] See Barthes, op. cit., pp. 79-80.

In Act III, when Oreste gives her the news that Pyrrhus has decided
to marry her after all, Hermione is still using the past to justify present
actions: 'Mais que puis-je, Seigneur? On a promis ma foi' (819). Feeling
she is on safe ground, she can claim that she would indeed have
followed him, had not duty dictated otherwise. Oreste does nonetheless
see through this obvious deceit: 'Ah! que vous saviez bien, cruelle [...]'
(827). Following another cruel rejection by Pyrrhus, she finally reveals
to Oreste the truth about her love, proving that there must have indeed
been an ulterior motive for her earlier denials.

> Je ne m'en cache point: l'ingrat m'avait su plaire,
> Soit qu'ainsi l'ordonnât mon amour ou mon père. (1193-5)

This comparative sincerity at this juncture does not stretch far enough
to prevent her from adducing a new argument: the future, the threat of
an imminent and brutal reversion to her old love: 'S'il ne meurt
aujourd'hui, je puis l'aimer demain' (1200). Her final exploitation of the
past comes when, in order to gain her own personal revenge over
Pyrrhus, she uses the hatred of the Greeks for the Trojans to arm her
men against him. Like Pyrrhus, her attempts to manipulate the past
backfire. Her plans result in the death of the man she loves and,
overcome with grief, she takes her own life. Hermione uses the past at
every opportunity to manipulate people and situations. Her devotion to
the past is indeed strong, in so far as it is consistent with her present
desires. When it can no longer be of any use to her, the true extent of
this devotion is revealed:

> Je renonce à la Grèce, à Sparte, à son empire,
> A toute ma famille [...] (1562-3)

For all her scheming, however, Hermione cannot outdo Pyrrhus for
the most despicable use of the past. Having cruelly rejected her for a
second time, he tries to extricate himself from the responsibilities he
knows he has by saying that while a lesser man might remind her that
theirs was a marriage arranged in the past by their fathers, without the
consent of either, he would of course never stoop so low.

> Un autre vous diroit que dans les champs troyens
> Nos deux pères sans nous formèrent ces liens,
> Et que sans consulter ni mon choix ni le vôtre,
> Nous fûmes sans amour engagés l'un à l'autre;
> Mais c'est assez pour moi que je me sois soumis. (1283-7)

Hermione remains unimpressed. While for her the past is held in high esteem as long as it supports her present desires, for Pyrrhus it can be undermined when present circumstances have changed.

Even on the evidence produced in this short article, we can see that the past is neither static nor simple. Throughout the play the past influences the development of the plot in two ways. This juxtaposition, as we have seen, introduces a subtle irony. Pyrrhus and Hermione use time as a pretext, a justification for present action, a strategic device or as evidence in an argument. Time therefore forms an essential part of the structure of the plot. The limited power this gives the protagonists is vastly outweighed by the underlying power which the past has, in a very real sense, over all of them. Pyrrhus cannot, despite all his efforts, control the past. He cannot negate his crimes, nor can he wipe out Andromaque's memory of Hector. Even his own words are often made to work against him. Andromaque's attempts to use the past strategically may be fruitless, but these pale into insignificance in the face of the overwhelming power her past has over Pyrrhus. One part of the discovery we as spectators make is an awareness of just how little control we have over the influence of the past in our own lives.

Bérénice: tragedy or anti-tragedy?

BY

RICHARD PARISH

ST. CATHERINE'S COLLEGE, OXFORD

Bérénice, qui [...] est si emportée dans le commencement et dans tous les cinq actes, [devient] tout-à-coup de sens rassis pour dénouer et finir la pièce, quand elle a assez duré, et donne le bon soir à Titus et à la compagnie par un simple changement de volonté: je ne m'y attendais pas, je l'avoue; j'ai trouvé cela nouveau, et de plus de fort bon exemple.

Thus the abbé de Villars in 1671 accurately expressing, as he so often does, the most salient difficulties of interpretation in *Bérénice*.

This paper addresses this one simple question, which has undergone many formulations beginning with the immediate reaction which I have just quoted, through the succeeding generations of commentators on the play, and which is based on the objection that *Bérénice* offers no resolution of the catharsis, because no release is afforded by the death of any of the characters—none of what Barnwell writes of in terms of 'tranquillity of mind'[1] and 'joy and relief' (p. 249). If we assume that the purgation of pity and terror, whatever form it may take, needs to culminate in a release from these feelings at the end of the play by the removal of their cause, *Bérénice* must appear problematic, in distinction to the majority of plays of Racine where the major protagonists die.

My starting point is to suggest that, more than any other Racinian tragedy, *Bérénice* is a play about the Roman exemplification of 'gloire'. However, there are two paradoxes which accompany the fulfilment of this ideal. The first, and one that Titus would be willing to embrace, is what we might call creative self-destruction, whereby the individual risks being destroyed, but the ideal subsists. The secondary paradox, however, whose terms Titus rejects, lies in the wounding of that same individual whose approval would not only be the object of his 'glorieux' exploits, but is in his case situated at the very origin of his adoption of a noble ethos, and of the actions which have affirmed it. Bérénice, in distinction to her Suetonian model, has formed Titus in every positive respect—she has, in other words, allowed him to aspire to his 'gloire'—

---

[1] H.T. Barnwell, *The Tragic Drama of Corneille and Racine* (Oxford 1982), p. 220.

and yet, as Sussman comments, 'it is the fundamental irony of the play that Bérénice first made the emperor aware of his responsibility to the people who now reject her';[2] or Hubert: 'Titus, pour rester complètement fidèle à Bérénice, doit donc l'exiler'.[3]

There is then in this play a common, and animate, middle denominator, which unites the achievements of noble deeds with the suppression of personal feeling in such a way as to necessitate the infliction of suffering on this third entity. This is a paradox which would, in the terms of the Cornelian ethos, serve only to enhance the status of the 'gloire' achieved; and Paulin is its unhesitating spokesman in such lines to Titus, anticipating the judgement of posterity, as:

> Songez, en ce malheur,
> Quelle gloire va suivre un moment de douleur,
> Quels applaudissements l'univers vous prépare,
> Quel rang dans l'avenir [...] (1209-12)[4]

We might call this secondary paradox that ensues, what Titus refers to as 'ce cruel sacrifice' (471), that of the punished saviour, and it is made explicit in Titus's oxymoronic appeal to Bérénice in IV, v: 'Vous-même, contre vous, fortifiez mon cœur' (1054). It is in this secondary paradox, however, that we find the dimension of 'gloire' that is rejected morally by Titus ('C'est peu d'être constant, il faut être barbare' (992)). As Defaux remarks, 'Titus recognizes that his duty has made him guilty, that it has forced him to become monstrous in his ingratitude and cruelty'.[5]

This is perhaps the point at which to cast doubt on Barthes's hypothesis that Rome serves as a pretext for an action Titus wishes to take: 'Titus n'est lié à Bérénice que par l'habitude [...]. Rome, avec ses lois qui défendent jalousement la pureté de son sang, est une instance toute désignée pour autoriser l'abandon de Bérénice'.[6] We must on occasion doubt the motives of Titus, as does Bérénice; but, as does Bérénice, we must finally concede the *bona fides* of Titus as he concludes his monologue in V, vi. Bérénice's 'Hélas!' which interrupts it is the sign of her conversion to a belief in Titus's love, and one to which the reader / spectator whom she in some sense represents on stage is thus also committed. Nor does the deliberate *dépoétisation* of Titus in

---

[2] R. Sussman, '*Bérénice* and the Tragic Moment', in *Esprit Créateur*, 15 (1975), 241-51 (p. 248).

[3] J.D. Hubert, *Essai d'exégèse racinienne* (Paris, 1985), p. 37.

[4] Quotations from Racine are taken from *Œuvres complètes*, L'Intégrale (Paris, 1962). Unless otherwise indicated line references are to *Bérénice*. Quotations from Corneille are taken from *Œuvres complètes*, L'Intégrale (Paris, 1963).

[5] G. Defaux, 'The Case of Bérénice: Racine, Corneille and Mimetic Desire', in *Yale French Studies*, 76 (1989), 211-39 (p. 219).

[6] R. Barthes, *Sur Racine* (Paris, 1963), pp. 94, 98.

the Act II encounter betoken his lack of feeling. On the contrary, it is his strength of feeling which prevents him from taking the risk of expressive speech. He is, in his own words to Antiochus, 'un *amant* interdit'. As Hubert comments more helpfully: 'Le but de l'empereur dès le début de la pièce, ce n'est pas de garder Bérénice auprès de lui, mais [...] de lui faire comprendre la situation aussi glorieuse que désespérée où ils se trouvent tous les deux' (p. 44).

Titus is thus prepared to sacrifice himself or indeed to die for Rome, (he is adamant that he should not become 'Un indigne empereur sans empire, sans cour' (1405)), and is not far from doing so at the play's conclusion. Faced with this dilemma, he will, in the closing stages of the play, declare himself ready to commit suicide:

> Il est, vous le savez, une plus noble voie;
> Je me suis vu, madame, enseigner ce chemin,
> Et par plus d'un héros, et par plus d'un Romain (1408-10)

Even if we note that at this stage, far from doing so in the pursuit of 'gloire', he is doing so because he is being pursued by it ('Ma gloire inexorable à toute heure me suit' (1394)), a complete reversal of the Cornelian pattern. As Barnwell comments: '[Titus's] concept of glory is negative and itself a burden to be shouldered' (p. 60). The solution he finally envisages thus necessarily accepts death, but seeks (impossibly) to reject the corollary that Bérénice's suffering will contribute to his posthumous status.

Awareness of these paradoxes is acute in the speeches both of Titus and, later, Bérénice herself. The secondary paradox is indeed exploited manipulatively by her as she draws attention implicitly to the inherent perversity in the Cornelian idea that love is expressed through, and yet despite, the infliction of suffering, endorsing her taunt: 'Êtes-vous pleinement content de votre gloire?' (1331) with the highly concentrated line: 'Ah! cruel, par pitié, montrez-moi moins d'amour' (1350).

If, therefore, in the light of this evidence, death had been the outcome of *Bérénice*, the play would still have constituted a critique of 'gloire', but one expressed in terms of the triumph of 'gloire'. And, it cannot be over-stressed, it needs very little for such an emphasis to conclude the action. At the beginning of Bérénice's last tirade, that is a mere thirty-seven lines before the play ends, the deaths of Titus, of Antiochus, and of Bérénice are prepared: 'glorieux' values will, it appears, prevail after all, and in spite of the mental reservations of Titus. It is as if everything Bérénice has striven for in terms of reforming the moral outlook of Titus has taken on its own dynamic within the Roman ethos, and is enhanced by the epiphanic adoption of his status as emperor (1096-8), only to reach a conclusion in the rejection of its creator, Bérénice.

Death at this stage in the play would confirm such a Roman interpretation; and it would furthermore provide the conditions for a catharsis which would be entirely straightforward and conventional. There would, in the words of the Preface, be 'du sang et des morts'; indeed Bérénice in her last tirade remarks: 'Je ne vois que des pleurs, et je n'entends parler / Que de trouble, d'horreurs, de sang prêt à couler' (1473-4). These 'horreurs' would endorse a tragic ethos whereby the 'gloire' of Titus was ratified by his death, in spite of his distancing himself from what I have called the secondary paradox, because affording a perfect expression of the primary one. Racine would have written a Roman tragedy, whose dénouement would be entirely in accord with the moral expectations aroused, with conventional criteria for catharsis, and indeed with the ostensible direction of the play's development over the best part of five acts. And it is by stressing the closeness of the leading trio to suicide that Racine places in particularly high relief the motivation of Bérénice in rejecting it, in staunching the bloody dénouement.

But Bérénice the queen is not herself Roman, and therein lies the problem, since *Bérénice* the play, (significantly differently entitled from its Cornelian counterpart), cannot be either: 'Rome, par une loi qui ne se peut changer, / N'admet avec son sang aucun sang étranger' (377-8). She is rather the exemplification of what Batache-Watt describes, when she comments that 'la plupart des héroïnes raciniennes ne sont, en réalité, que des étrangères isolées dans des pays peu accueillants';[7] and indeed Greenberg goes as far as to describe Bérénice as one of 'Classicism's misfits'.[8] The race, and indeed sex, of Bérénice the queen modify the genre of *Bérénice* the play. Gender and genre are closely dependent. So when the Palestinian queen gets up, in a last supreme effort, to speak her final words, she does two things: she re-interprets retrospectively the significance of all that has so far taken place in the play; and she re-situates it in the context of the tragic genre. Why, and how, does she do this?

What Bérénice crucially appeals to in her conclusion is the idea of examplarity, and in so doing reflects closely, indeed in one sense replies to, the words spoken by Titus in IV, v, after the enumeration of precedents (to whom the initial 'Malheureux!' in the following quotation makes reference):

> Malheureux! Mais toujours la patrie et la gloire
> Ont parmi les Romains remporté la victoire.

---

[7] E. Batache-Watt, *Profils des héroïnes raciniennes* (Paris, 1976), p. 91.

[8] M. Greenberg, '*L'Astrée*, Classicism and the Illusion of Modernity', in *Continuum*, 2 (1990), 1-25 (p. 3).

> Je sais qu'en vous quittant le malheureux Titus
> Passe l'austérité de toutes leurs vertus;
> Qu'elle n'approche point de cet effort insigne:
> Mais, madame, après tout, me croyez-vous indigne
> De laisser un exemple à la postérité,
> Qui, sans de grands efforts, ne puisse être imité? (1167-74)

It is then soon developed: first of all in Titus's quatrain beginning: 'Je n'aurai pas, madame, à compter tant de jours' (1122-5); and then, unmistakably understood in terms of suicide by both Titus and Bérénice in V, vi, before he hands over morally and rhetorically to her the obligation to decide on their lives or deaths:

> En l'état où je suis je puis tout entreprendre:
> Et je ne réponds pas que ma main à vos yeux
> N'ensanglante à la fin nos funestes adieux. (1420-2)

The 'exemple' of IV, v, then, consists of respecting the imperatives of 'gloire' in such a way that, when the lines of Bérénice are spoken at the end of the play, these imperatives have been interpreted in terms of an imminent suicide pact.

It should also be stressed that suicide, for Titus, is not the ignoble solution, but rather the imitation of the aristocratic, indeed Roman paradigm: it is the example, *par excellence*, or will be perceived as such, of aristocratic conduct pursued *in extremis*, an example that will have been transmitted to Titus 'Et par plus d'un héros et par plus d'un Romain'. Racine thus already underlines the fundamental difference between his protagonists and those of Corneille; and, by presenting suicide as noble and as Roman, he offers it also as inevitable. It is above all this insistence that places the emphasis on the motives of Bérénice in rejecting it. For Corneille, suicide is easily rejected as an unworthy act: when Tite proposes suicide as one of three possibilities, (the others being exile and marriage, both of which are equally rejected by Racine's Titus), it is immediately dismissed by Bérénice:

> Non, Seigneur, ce n'est pas aux Reines comme moi
> A hasarder leurs jours pour signaler leur foi.
> La plus illustre ardeur de périr l'un pour l'autre
> N'a rien de glorieux pour mon rang et le vôtre.
> (*Tite et Bérénice* (1009-12))

For Racine it is its very worthiness that seems to make of it a logical outcome, and which, in turn, directs our attention towards the terms of the epilogue which Bérénice pronounces at the end of the play. Because, if the emperor's suicide will unleash two others, since the whole exemplary trio will kill itself, then 'l'univers entier' will interpret the deaths of Antiochus and of Bérénice in terms of further sacrifices on the altar of Roman 'gloire'. In this way, therefore, Bérénice, in replying to Titus, is again taking upon herself the moral decision, establishing the ethos of their acts, and thus of the play. Her very last lines to Titus are in fact the direct answer to Titus's transferral of responsibility at the end of V, vi: 'Vous voilà de nos jours maintenant responsable. / Songez-y bien, madame: et si je vous suis cher ...' (1424-5).

When she addresses the 'princes trop généreux' in her final speech, therefore, we may well feel that Bérénice is using the term with all its traditional, indeed archaic, resonances of *generosus*, 'well-born', and thus with its related appeal to the example of aristocratic values. They are 'too noble'. And the tragic effect that would be created by the sacrifice proposed, however reluctant, on the altar of Roman 'gloire' may also be deemed archaic, or at the very least conventional. The spectator would be released by the cessation of suffering of the three protagonists, and either uplifted or saddened (or filled with *admiration*) by their ultimate defeat at the hands of an order which transcends personal claims.

But Bérénice subverts this tragic commonplace on the very verge of the dénouement. By beginning the last few lines of her speech: 'Adieu. Servons tous trois d'exemples à l'univers' she is simply drawing attention to a status which is already accorded to them by definition, given the fame of Rome, and the weight of their responsibility towards it. But what is not predetermined is its significance, let alone the implications of that significance. Thus as Bérénice concludes her speech:

> Adieu. Servons tous trois d'exemples à l'univers
> De l'amour la plus tendre et la plus malheureuse
> Dont il puisse garder l'histoire douloureuse [...] (1502-4)

she invites the exemplary trio to accept separation, and to reject death. And, crucially, she does this because dying serves 'gloire'; remaining alive allows their exemplary act to be recorded as being at the service of the mutual love that they all have for each other. Furthermore the love triangle in this play is perfect: between Bérénice and Titus; between Bérénice and Antiochus; but also between the two male protagonists as well, as Antiochus finally reveals in his lines to Titus: 'Vous m'avez malgré moi confié, l'un et l'autre, / La reine, son amour, et vous, seigneur, le vôtre' (1435-6). It is this triangle which will expand into the trio of exemplary renunciation. Thus in choosing to live, they are choosing, at the instigation of the foreign queen Bérénice, the anti-'glorieux' option. And at the instigation of a woman, they are rejecting the 'passions plus nobles et plus mâles que l'amour' of Cornelian theory.

Defaux formulates this admirably, when he writes that 'the struggle that
takes place in Titus is not so much a struggle between Duty and Love as
one between the Woman and the Father' (p. 234).

Before looking at the generic implications of this, I should consider
briefly here a further parallel with *Tite et Bérénice*, since the way in
which Corneille handles his dénouement also throws a particularly
helpful light on the reading of Racine's solution to the absence of deaths
(and, let it be said, it would not presumably have been out of the
question for either dramatist, but especially Racine, to feel that
vraisemblance demanded that deaths be introduced into the plot). The
intermediate option of remaining alive yet still serving as 'glorieux'
examples, the option that is chosen by Corneille, is not however even
entertained by Bérénice at this stage of Racine's play. Such a solution
would be more in accordance with the understanding of catharsis which
assumes it may derive from the Cornelian criterion of *admiration*,
thereby removing the problem of the need for a release from pity and
terror, and circumventing the difficulty of a bloodless dénouement.
Corneille's play, (generically sub-titled 'comédie héroïque'), differs
fundamentally therefore in the ideological ethos of its dénouement
(particularly between V, iv and the end). Bérénice exhorts Tite to
behave in a 'glorieux' way in order to retain her love, a
characteristically Cornelian expression of 'dignité' (*Tite et Bérénice*
1639-46). It is then learnt that the senate in fact approves Tite's
marriage to Bérénice, allowing him to rejoice: 'Grâces au juste ciel, ma
gloire en sûreté / N'a plus à redouter aucune indignité' (*Tite et Bérénice*
1677-8). This however leads Bérénice not to consent, but to renounce
Tite, arguing thereby for the values of Rome:

> Rome a sauvé ma gloire en me donnant sa voix,
> Sauvons-lui, vous et moi, la gloire de ses lois,
> Rendons-lui, vous et moi, cette reconnaissance
> D'en avoir pour vous plaire affaibli la puissance [...]
> (*Tite et Bérénice* (1697-1700))

This is in order that posterity should not be set a dangerous precedent,
incurring the risk that 'D'autres sur votre exemple épouseraient des
reines / Qui n'auraient pas, Seigneur, des âmes si romaines' (*Tite et
Bérénice* (1703-4)). On this exaltation of 'gloire', and content in the
knowledge that 'Votre cœur est à moi, j'y règne, c'est assez' (*Tite et
Bérénice* (1714)), Bérénice leaves, confident that history will keep, in
Tite's words, 'l'illustre souvenir' (*Tite et Bérénice* (1758)) of their
example.

Three recent critical reactions might serve to resume the opposition
between the two plays. Barnwell writes: 'Whereas Racine's tragedy is

that of passionate and guiltless love frustrated by an inescapable but repugnant duty, Corneille's play concerns the willing acceptance of a duty which brings its own satisfactions in its train and, through the renunciation of marriage, allows the characters to achieve their "gloire"' (p. 57). Siguret, studying rhyme patterns in the two tragedies, concludes that '*Bérénice* [...] raconte un *sacrifice* intime, écrasant et injuste' whereas '*Tite et Bérénice* [raconte] une justice héroïque rendue aux autres et à soi-même'.[9] Finally, for Defaux, Racine's play has a 'confrontational nature', since his 'dramatic aesthetic is nothing else, in its very essence, than the [...] inversion of Corneille's aesthetic' (p. 213). Far from being Racine's most Cornelian tragedy, *Bérénice* is the tragedy in which the Cornelian ethos is most explicitly rejected.

When appraising the ideological significance of the final tirade, we must equally take into account considerations of *genre*. The refusal of death, its refutation as an exemplary act, explicitly rejects this authentification of Roman and 'glorieux' values, and, at the same time, necessarily disallows the kind of dénouement which conventionally expresses it. By her re-interpretation of the values of the play, Bérénice also makes inevitable a re-categorization of the limits of the play, and thus of the genre, of so radical a kind that we might indeed be tempted to talk in terms of an anti-tragedy. Since the superficial subject matter of the play remains Roman, (its primary business is the dilemma of the emperor confronted with the hostility of Rome towards the woman he would seek to marry), the character of the play's dénouement could have been expected to reflect the cathartic effect (closer, even here, to *admiration* than to pity and terror) that the sacrifice to 'gloire' would provoke. So, since death is excluded by definition, or at least by the terms of the *inventio*, from the dénouement of *Bérénice*, we find ourselves confronted with the rather tired question: is the dénouement of *Bérénice* tragic? I will attempt to find a rather less tired answer.

Let us first of all forget the debased meaning of the term, unhelpfully encouraged by Racine in his Preface: yes, of course, it's sad, but the assertion of the play's 'tristesse majestueuse' just leaves to one side the most difficult questions, *pace* Vinaver, who writes: 'Cette tristesse, est-elle en effet autre chose que l'état de sérénité devant le fait tragique, le recueillement de l'âme qui, pure de tout trouble, s'ouvre à l'intelligence des actes humains et des lois suprêmes dont ils portent l'image?'[10] (to which the simple answer is, yes it is). Biard also expresses a rather genteel unease with the Preface: 'Le fait que cette nouvelle définition du tragique soit de la plume d'un dramaturge dont l'œuvre abonde en

---

[9] F. Siguret, 'Bérénice / Impératrice: lecture d'une rime', in *French Forum*, 3 (1978), 125-31 (pp. 130-31).

[10] E. Vinaver, *Racine et la poésie tragique* (Paris, 1951) p. 46.

meurtres, suicides et autres issues fatales est assez remarquable',[11] but
does not proceed therefrom to challenge its terms. Nor does it initially
help to think of the continued existence of the figures as a kind of
'living death', worse than a true death (in one reading at least of such
lines as Phèdre's 'Est-ce un malheur si grand que de cesser de vivre?'
(868)). This again may be true, and finds critical expression in
Dainard's article, for example, when he writes of 'death or, in *Bérénice*,
its equivalent, exile',[12] but it still does not go to the root of the problem.

The starting point for a possible interpretation of this dénouement
will in fact be a very simple observation. Bérénice, alone among
Racine's heroes and heroines, says at the end of the play that she will
leave, and then leaves of her own free will: 'Tout est prêt; on m'attend.
Ne suivez point mes pas' (1505). In so doing she is exercising a
freedom, the 'droit de sortie', normally reserved, as Barthes points out
(p. 61), for confidants. In thus leaving, Bérénice deprives the audience
of her presence, just as death would (a point that is notably true in a
theatrical aesthetic wherein death is never, or rarely, seen on the stage,
so that there is no mimetic expectation); and she does this by uniquely
breaking the power of the magnetic space that the stage is, or has
become, in the course of the play. The release from the catharsis is
effected, therefore, first of all at the theatrical level, rather than the
moral or aesthetic, by this movement from the stage. Since death itself
is a kind of departure, the departure in *Bérénice* from the stage
produces a similar kind of release, because an imprisonment is broken.
As the audience is released by the breaking out of other tragic figures
from their mortal dilemma, (whether or not the characters themselves
may be considered so to be released), so it is here by the breaking of the
spatial magnetism that an equivalent effect is produced. This theatrical
release, however, points as well to a rejection of the kind of catharsis
implied by 'gloire', that is, a catharsis deriving from death, as the
primary, 'glorieux' paradox of creative self-destruction is replaced by
its complementary paradox, that of sterile survival (and that is why,
although we may accurately talk of a 'living death', its significance
should not be confused with that of a 'dying death', since Racine's
dénouement directly contradicts it).

What such a reversal releases us from is thus far more fundamental,
since it releases us from a particular convention of tragedy, and from
the values that such a convention expresses. As Bérénice walks out on a
conventional dénouement, we are not purged of sexual passions by the
release of death (and the denial of death and the denial of sexual
fulfilment are both in one sense refusals of a release). What we are

---

[11] J.-D. Biard, 'Le Ton élégiaque dans *Bérénice*', in *French Studies*, 19 (1965), 1-15 (p. 2).

[12] J. Dainard, 'The Power of the Spoken Word in *Bérénice*', in *Romanic Review*, 67 (1976), 157-71 (p. 159).

rather purged of by the refusal of the sacrificial death of Bérénice on a Roman altar, and by her leaving the stage, are again the 'passions plus nobles et plus mâles que l'amour': imperialism, heroism, and self-fulfilment, as exemplified by the Roman ethos. By drawing our attention to an expectation, Racine thus reminds us of conventions both of form and of substance; but by breaking down those conventions, he places the resultant awareness of the limits of the genre at the service both of his theatrical conception and of his ideological concerns.

It is thus with the greatest scepticism that we should confront the preface, dated a year later than the first performance of the play which it is supposed to introduce, but which seems to reply so efficiently to certain problems of definition which the tragic genre presents:

> ... ce n'est point une nécessité qu'il y ait du sang et des morts dans une tragédie: il suffit que l'action en soit grande, que les acteurs en soient héroïques, que les passions y soient excitées, et que tout s'y ressente de cette tristesse majestueuse qui fait tout le plaisir de la tragédie.

Is this a definition of tragedy in general? Or isn't it rather a defence, *ex post facto*, of one tragedy in particular? The preface to *Bérénice* would more accurately be described as a postface, and one in which the dogmatic *sententiae* with which it confronts the reader are transparently disingenuous. It is in this respect that *Bérénice* is an anti-tragedy; because the terms of the dénouement show how, behind these very claims of orthodoxy, is hidden an unambiguous statement of theatrical, political, and indeed sexual iconoclasm.

Phèdre's Guilt:
a theatrical reading

J<small>AMES</small> J. S<small>UPPLE</small>

UNIVERSITY OF ST ANDREWS

In her much-quoted *Lire le théâtre*, Anne Ubersfeld argues that reading the text of a play is an inadequate way of experiencing it—but that there is no escape. Individual performances are, by their nature, transitory: and even the director and actors must use the text as their starting point. Writing as a semiologist, she defines the 'message' which the performed play produces as a combination of Text (T) and Performance (P): 'Message = T + P'.[1] Her approach often produces real insights, but, like all such approaches, does tend to be overly abstract.[2] She is obviously right to satirise the view that Racine's theatre should be read like 'un vaste poème' (p. 8), as though reading *Phèdre* were no different from reading the Dido and Æneas episode in the *Æneid*. One wonders, however, whether a more sophisticated approach to reading the text *as a script* might not enable one better to appreciate its theatrical implications.

Few academics ever experience *Phèdre* in a way which directly corresponds to the T + P formula. In this case, Ubersfeld's *émetteur* ('auteur + metteur en scène + autres praticiens + comédiens', p. 37) will have to be extended to include the members of the audience who, as former readers of the text, have their own sometimes similar, sometimes different view of it. Another way of putting this is that the spectators concerned respond not only to the text as mediated by the performance, but also in an unmediated way as a result of their own memories of the text (and, of course, of other performances). The 'message' in this case should be represented thus: $(T + P) + T^R$, where T^R represents the text as read / remembered by the spectators. This will often result in 'interferences' as $(T + P)$ and T^R clash. Thus, if Act II, scene v were performed in the way suggested by Claudel, with

---

[1] *Lire le théâtre* (Paris, 1982), p. 37.

[2] See, for example, the schemas concerning *Phèdre* (pp. 88-9), and J. Lempert, *'Phèdre' de Racine: pour une sémiotique de la représentation classique* (Paris, 1972).

Hippolyte being attracted to Phèdre,[3] the present writer would immediately wonder how the director was going to deal with what seems to be an evident retrospective stage direction given by Phèdre in Act III scene i: 'Comme il ne respirait qu'une retraite prompte!' (745). One of the main advantages of this kind of unusual presentation of well known plays is, of course, to jolt spectators into reassessing their *idées fixes*.[4] This can sometimes be achieved by a brilliant critic, Barthes for instance.[5] However, confronted with some critics' elaborations upon the theatrical experience, one can appreciate why some directors are tempted to reject 'toute exégèse universitaire' as 'inutile et pesante'.[6] Ironically, this may often be the case when the literary critics believe they are making an allowance for the particular nature of the theatrical experience. Thus, Constant Venesoen is quite right to argue that *Phèdre* is constructed in a way which is designed to stimulate the audience's emotions; but I cannot accept the suggestion that, though Phèdre's final speech is obviously misleading,[7] 'un public "réagissant"' will have no time for 'des finasseries psychologiques, réservées, le cas échéant, au lecteur pointilleux'.[8] Geoffrey Brereton makes a similarly misguided point in his analysis of the crucial scene in Act III in which Phèdre allows Œnone to accuse Hippolyte of attempted rape. He mentions some of the attenuating circumstances and highlights her subsequent desire to save her victim in Act IV, but comments: 'these attenuations are not enough. In spite of them, Phèdre might still appear odious to an audience which is not, while in the theatre, in a position to weigh with care the psychological circumstances surrounding the act, but sees chiefly the act and its consequences'.[9] No audience will be attempting to 'weigh anything with care' in Act III, but it will have *witnessed* Phèdre's panic when told not only that Thésée is alive but that his return is imminent. It will have *heard* her say she fears to see how Hippolyte, 'le témoin de [sa] flamme adultère', will react when she has to greet his father (840-2). It will have *seen* her horror at Œnone's suggested solution ('Moi, que j'ose opprimer et noircir l'innocence!', (893)), and then her almost immediate collapse as Hippolyte enters with Thésée (909-12). Even if the impact of all this were at a largely pre-

---

[3] Quoted in B. Croquette (ed.), *Racine: 'Phèdre'* (Paris, 1988), p. 111.

[4] Claudel's approach could be made to work if Hippolyte was gradually made to become more and more attracted to Phèdre but to recoil at the end of the labyrinth speech.

[5] *Sur Racine* (Paris, 1960).

[6] Ubersfeld, p. 7.

[7] See below p. 123.

[8] *Jean Racine et le procès de la culpabilité* (Paris, 1981), p. 189.

[9] *Jean Racine. A Critical Biography* (London, 1951), p. 226.

logical level, it would still leave the spectator graphically aware of the extenuating circumstances.

It would seem that some Racine critics might well reflect further on what is involved in a theatrical experience before making such hard and fast judgments on it. This wisdom of this is illustrated by Thierry Maulnier's original study of *Phèdre* published in 1943: 'Seule protagoniste, Phèdre rejette à l'arrière-plan les autres héros qui ne sont plus que des comparses [...]'.[10] This conflicts totally with Jean-Louis Barrault's experience as director: '*Phèdre* n'est pas un concerto pour femme; c'est une symphonie pour orchestre d'acteurs'.[11] More interestingly, it also conflicts with Maulnier's experience some twenty years later of actually staging the play (p. 139):

> ... le critique a la liberté d'éliminer dédaigneusement de son propos, de réduire du moins à une fonction abstraite, à une immatérialité d'ombres, des personnages secondaires. Pour le metteur en scène, ces personnages sont là, ils ont leur place à tenir, leur épaisseur charnelle d'existants à assurer sur le théâtre [...] Aussi ai-je bien été forcé de découvrir qu'il y avait dans Œnone bien sûr, mais aussi dans Hippolyte, dans Aricie elle-même, plus de ressources et de replis qu'il ne m'avait paru d'abord.

The semiologist would argue, of course, that such a character-centred statement ignores the properly theatrical dimension of the play, since many of the various sign systems can only interact properly—can only exist—when the play is performed. Seen in this light, Racine's theatre has sometimes been spurned as epitomising the view of those who feel that 'le théâtre est avant tout un texte littéraire, accessoirement agrémenté par une mise en scène illustrante'.[12] Recently, however, three British scholars have reacted against this view, either implicitly (Richard Parish) or explicitly: Henry Phillips and David Maskell. Parish analyses very intelligently the way in which Racine's text exploits both implicit and explicit stage directions and, indeed, how it serves to indicate and define the theatrical space in which the play takes place.[13] Phillips, again concentrating on speech, insists nonetheless on its theatricality, arguing in particular that 'it is possible to reconstruct a thematics of speech and listening which commands all aspects of the theatrical dimension'.[14] Maskell, finally, provides the first systematic

---

[10] *Lecture de Phèdre* (Paris, 1967), p. 139.

[11] Quoted in Croquette, p. 19.

[12] P. Davis, *Problèmes de sémiologie théâtrale* (Montreal, 1976), p. 11.

[13] 'Racine: scène et vers', in C. Hill (ed.), *Racine: théâtre et poésie* (Leeds, 1991), pp. 139-50.

[14] 'Racinian Tragedy: Text as Theatre', in E. Forman (ed.), *Racine: Appraisal and Reappraisal* (Bristol, 1991), pp. 25-37.

study of Racine's theatricality: *Racine. A Theatrical Reading.*[15] This is not a guide on how to stage Racine: it is, as its title suggests, a reading of the plays in which the author looks meticulously for all those clues which show that Racine was a man of the theatre rather than a poet who happened to write plays. Thus he shows how Phèdre's horror at her passion is epitomised by her difficulty in walking, by her sitting down, and by the possibility of her loosening her hair (p. 200); how the celebrated reference to the decor (855-7) takes on its full value as Phèdre feels that even the vaults above her will denounce her (p. 202); and how the pressure on her increases in Act III, scene iv as Thésée enters accompanied by two other men (Hippolyte is accompanied by Théramène), thus symbolising in theatrical terms how exposed the 'delinquent female' must have felt.[16]

Although my subtitle is taken from Maskell's book, I hope to develop his approach in two different ways. Firstly, by applying it directly to the traditionally vexed question of Phèdre's guilt;[17] and, secondly, by emphasising the discrepancy implicit in Racine's script concerning elements which are clearly indicated by the author and those which are deliberately left vague. Modern direc ors will often insist on the right to free themselves from what Ubersfeld calls 'le terrorisme textuel' (p. 8) and to produce a play in a free, creative way. There are, however, two points to be made about the status of Racine's text as a script. First, even if many literary critics seem to be ill equipped to deal with the theatrical experience as such, their attempts at interpreting the text must approximate in some degree to those of professional *metteurs en scène*—who will also have to interpret their script before they attempt to stage it. Even the most renowned literary critics are capable of making the most aberr nt statements;[18] but their famous disagreements often serve to highlight the ambiguities of the script. Second, however much an individual director may attempt to respect the essential ambiguity of Racine's characters,[19] the very fact of putting them on stage, of making them dress, speak, behave and interact in a particular way will automatically reduce the degree of ambiguity. As we read the script, we can, on the other hand, imagine the advantages or disadvantages of following Maulnier and visualising a youngish Phèdre (pp. 59 ff.), or of following Jean Pommier and casting for an older

---

[15] Oxford, 1991.

[16] Pp. 62-3. I develop somewhat what I take to be the implications of his argument.

[17] Maskell makes several relevant comments (e.g. pp. 200-201).

[18] See Picard (below pp. 120-21).

[19] See P. France's excellent comments in *Jean Racine: 'Andromaque'* (Glasgow, 1989), pp. 18 ff.

woman.[20] The director, however, has to choose a particular actress.[21] A younger Phèdre will feel more affronted that Hippolyte prefers Aricie to her (Maulnier, pp. 66-7). An older woman might leave some spectators feeling as Pommier does (pp. 210-11) that falling in love with a young man 'qui pourrait être son fils' constitutes a kind of psychological incest of much more import than the 'demi-inceste' involved in falling in love with your stepson.

Critics have noted the fact that, whereas many of his predecessors (Gilbert and Bidar for instance) avoided any suggestion of incest, Racine deliberately constructed his plot in a way which would highlight this issue.[22] However, the absence of blood ties makes it far from clear-cut. Some feel, nonetheless, that any debate on this issue is irrelevant. Clause Abraham argues, for instance:

> Another common error is that of critics who debate Phèdre's guilt according to Hellenic, Roman, or Gallic laws.[23] Phèdre is not guilty of incest because of a law or innocent because of another; she is guilty because she considers herself so. She states it quite clearly when she asks 'How can the widow of Theseus love his son?' (702)[24]

Pat Short is of like mind,[25] as is Barry Kite (p. 70). Raymond Picard makes a similar point, but extends it to include all the other characters: 'il n'y a pas à proprement parler d'inceste, dans l'acception technique du terme, puisque Hippolyte n'est pas le fils de Phèdre. Peu importe: il suffit que tous les personnages considèrent que l'amour de Phèdre est incestueux'.[26] It is easy to sympathise with these critics since the effect on a performance of a decision concerning the objective reality (or otherwise) of Phèdre's 'incest' is likely to be minimal: Phèdre will be just as distraught whether she is incestuous or simply believes herself to be so. They overlook, however, the fact that they are not judging a legal point but studying characters in a particular dramatic context. Thésée, in his anger with Hippolyte, will regard the alleged attack on Phèdre as incestuous because it feeds his sense of outrage (1145-6). Hippolyte, similarly, will not hesitate to portray the crime as being as black as

---

[20] *Aspects de Racine* (Paris, 1954), pp. 207-11.

[21] We know from contemporary accounts that Racine was often very precise about the way in which his plays should be acted. When I refer to Racine's intentions here, I refer to his 'intentions' as deduced from his script. A script can obviously have a meaning other than that 'intended' by its author (Ubersfeld, p. 38).

[22] B. Kite, 'The Guilt of Phèdre: the Play and its Sources', in Forman, 67-81 (p. 69).

[23] The reference is probably to R.C. Knight, *Racine et la Grèce* (Paris, 1950), p. 340.

[24] *Jean Racine* (Boston, 1977), p. 124.

[25] *Racine: 'Phèdre'* (London, 1983), p. 36.

[26] In his edition of the *Œuvres* (Paris, 1966-8), vol. I, p. 738.

possible because it will enable him to contrast his virtuous behaviour with the alleged crime (1092-1113). Phèdre's judgment when she refers to her incest (1270, 1624) may also be no more than a reflection of the position in which she finds herself: lacerating herself because she feels that she has committed 'des crimes peut-être inconnus des enfers' (1284), or confessing her guilt to her husband. The anguished cry quoted by Abraham ('La veuve de Thésée ose aimer Hippolyte' (702)) is not, in itself, conclusive either, since it may well reflect Phèdre's sense of shame, which (though perfectly sincere) is obviously going to be accentuated by Hippolyte's evident horror at her confession. In these circumstances, it is significant that Racine has left us wondering about the exact nature of Phèdre's passion. In so far as we are not convinced that it is objectively incestuous, we will be inclined to admire Phèdre for her high moral standards.[27] This will, of course, make it easier for us to sympathise with the character we see suffering on the stage.

The question of the gods is similarly vexed. If Phèdre's passion has been visited on her by a malevolent deity, then the consequences of that passion cannot be totally ascribed to her. As Du Bos put it in 1719: 'Phèdre ne commet pas volontairement les crimes dont elle est punie; c'est un pouvoir divin auquel une mortelle ne saurait résister dans le système du paganisme, qui la force d'être incestueuse et perfide [...]; ses crimes ne paraissent plus être ses crimes que parce qu'elle en reçoit la punition. La haine en tombe sur Vénus'.[28] Venesoen adopts a very similar point of view in 1981, arguing that Phèdre 'est la victime antique, persécutée par les dieux' (p. 157), and quoting Racine's own preface: 'Elle est engagée, par sa destinée et par la colère des dieux, dans une passion illégitime, dont elle a horreur toute la première'.[29] This view is not universally held, however. Jacques Schérer, questioning 'la critique fataliste', argues that Phèdre is free, at any given moment, to act independently of any allegedly fixed destiny: 'A tout moment de la journée tragique, Phèdre était libre de refuser les conseils d'Œnone; cette journée n'est même tragique que parce que Phèdre y a choisi une direction qu'elle va bien vite condamner' (pp. 34-5). Picard adopts a similar position, rejecting the view that Phèdre might be regarded as a 'pantomime théologique, où les ficelles qui manœuvrent Phèdre, marionnette sacrée, seraient visibles aux yeux du spectateur exercé'. For him, the gods are no more than a pretext used by the protagonist to

---

[27] Schérer (p. 154) refers to her 'conscience morale exigeante'.

[28] Quoted in J. Salles's edition of the play (Paris, 1964), p. 73.

[29] P. 157. Venesoen regards Phèdre as being guilty, nonetheless, of 'une volonté de possession' (p. 163)—hence his criticisms of her. See below, *passim*.

justify her actions or, at best, 'la personnification de nos limites' (pp. 741-3). This view would have obvious consequences for staging: the setting and lighting would not suggest the presence of malevolent deities. Those holding the opposite view would, obviously, place a statue of Venus on stage in Act III, scene ii to receive Phèdre's prayer, or even replace Théramène with the figure of Neptune.[30] Which is more faithful to the spirit of the script? It is impossible to say: once again, Racine leaves us with an essential ambiguity.

So far, I have considered only general features of the play. What I would like to do now is to focus on elements of ambiguity in the plot. This ambiguity is present, though to a lesser degree, in both Act I and Act II;[31] but is more crucial from Act III on as Phèdre becomes involved in provoking Hippolyte's death. In most of what follows, I will restrict myself, therefore, to the final three acts. The false accusation of Hippolyte is the crux of the tragedy. Phèdre's first reflex when she learns of Thésée's return is to encourage suicide (835 ff). As in Act I, however, Œnone utilises her love of her children to prevent her from following her instincts (342 ff., 869-71), and then suggests accusing Hippolyte. It is sometimes argued that Phèdre is guilty of only 'une faiblesse presque innocente' (Picard, p. 739) and that she reproaches herself for crimes 'qu'elle ne commet qu'en imagination', and only then when 'les circonstances se conjurent pour les lui présenter sous les aspects les moins criminels' (Maulnier, p. 80). The audience watching Œnone working on Phèdre will note, however, that she quite unexpectedly jeopardises her chances of persuading her mistress by arguing that, though Thésée will probably only exile Hippolyte, the consequences of a false accusation might well be much more serious:

> Mais le sang innocent dût-il être versé,
> Que ne demande point votre honneur menacé? (903-4)

Bernard Weinberg is much nearer the mark, therefore, when he argues that 'Knowing this, Phèdre already assumes some moral responsibility when she agrees to have Œnone make the accusation'.[32]

---

[30] See Schérer, pp. 228-33.

[31] See Venesoen, pp. 162-4 on Act I, where he offers an unususal view of Phèdre ('Pressée par Œnone et avide d'exhaler cet amour qui lui brûle les lèvres et le corps [...]') and Act II (where he contrasts the interpretations offered by Picard and Barrault on the one hand and by Maulnier on the other).

[32] *The Art of Jean Racine* (Chicago, 1963), p. 264.

Members of an audience would also be more graphically aware than readers that Phèdre has rapidly moved from an apparently sincere and urgent rejection of such immoral behaviour to a position of almost total collapse:

> Ah! je vois Hippolyte;
> Dans ses yeux insolents je vois ma perte écrite.
> Fais ce que tu voudras, je m'abandonne à toi.
> Dans le trouble où je suis, je ne puis rien pour moi. (909-10)

This is less than twenty lines after the initial rejection of Œnone's plan; and might well justify Brereton's assertion that she is acting 'with a certain premeditation' and thus committing (or at least permitting) an 'act which goes beyond blind passion' (p. 226). Venesoen goes even further:

> Le retour de Thésée fait échec à la fureur de Phèdre. Hippolyte échappe au vœu de son amour, mais non à son emprise. Si Hippolyte ne peut pas lui appartenir, il n'appartiendra à personne, ni à Thésée ni à Aricie [...] Sacrifice de celui qu'on aime pour qu'il n'aime plus jamais. Infériorisation subtile, et fatale, qui consiste à détruire l'objet aimé afin que l'on soit, en détruisant, maître d'un destin. Tel est maintenant le projet de Phèdre, confus dans sa conception, à peine réfléchi, plus instinctif que volontaire, mais réel dans son exécution et dans ses effets. (p. 172)

It is rare for Phèdre to be presented as an almost Hermione-like figure, but such an interpretation could easily find support (see below pp. 118, 120, 123). Since the anguished cry 'Ah! je vois Hippolyte; / Dans ses yeux insolents je vois ma perte écrite' is immediately followed by what appears to be the signal for Œnone to go ahead with her plan ('Fais ce que tu voudras'), it would be easy to interpret the latter as a defensive reflex.

The signal is, however, only apparent. The reference to Hippolyte's 'yeux insolents' is definitely aggressive, but there is no proof in the script that this is the key element in Phèdre's decision to capitulate. She might be referring to her nightmare vision of having to watch Hippolyte watching her as she greets her husband, whose love for her she has betrayed (841-4). She might even be referring to her own expected inability to go through with it:

> Laissera-t-il trahir et son père et son roi?
> Pourra-t-il contenir l'horreur qu'il a pour moi?
> Il se tairait en vain. Je sais mes perfidies [...] (847-9)

If so; her concluding statement 'Dans le trouble où je suis, je ne puis rien pour moi' might well be an objective description of her emotional

and moral paralysis rather than a cynical excuse allowing her to give
Œnone permission to proceed. Even the famous 'Fais ce que tu voudras'
is potentially ambiguous. Anyone in a rational state of mind would
realise that Œnone will take this as acceptance of her plan; but there is
every reason to believe that Phèdre is not rational at this point. One
could argue that her failure to be specific is devious since it might be
seen as a manoeuvre designed to leave ultimate responsibility with her
nurse.[33] It is equally possible, on the other hand, that, having just
listened to Œnone's estimation of the fatal consequences to Hippolyte
(903-908), Phèdre is desperately hoping that she will think of another
way out—hence the use, perhaps, of the future tense of the verb *vouloir*
rather than the more explicit 'fais ce que tu veux', or even 'fais ce que
tu as dit'.

This interpretation would not remove Phèdre's responsibility for
giving Œnone permission to act on her behalf, but it would reduce it.
Although this is not necessarily the best interpretation: it is a *possible*
one, and, once again, Racine's script gives the director no clear clue as
to how the play should be produced.

The ambiguity extends into the next scene. Racine might well have
had Phèdre flee from the stage just as, or just before, Thésée enters.
Instead, he has her greet Thésée with the following words:

> Arrêtez, Thésée,
> Et ne profanez point des transports si charmants.
> Je ne mérite plus ces doux empressements.
> Vous êtes offensé. La fortune jalouse
> N'a pas en votre absence épargné votre épouse.
> Indigne de vous plaire et de vous approcher,
> Je ne dois désormais songer qu'à me cacher. (914-20)

The horrified Hippolyte wonders if Phèdre was not intending to
denounce herself (988-90), as indeed some of her words might seem to
suggest—'Je ne mérite plus ces doux empressements', for instance.
Obviously focussing on the part of the speech which might suggest that
she is a victim of someone else ('La fortune jalouse / N'a pas en votre
absence épargné votre épouse'), Dédéyan asks, on the other hand:
'Phèdre fait-elle ici le jeu d'Œnone?'. He points out that it is impossible
to say with certainty ('Nous ne saurions répondre, elle peut tout aussi
bien agir par scrupule moral que par calcul') before offering an honest
statement of what is merely his personal preference: 'Mais je penche
plutôt pour le scrupule'.[34] Weinberg also has doubts but seems to feel

[33] Venesoen, p. 174.

[34] *Racine: 'Phèdre'* (Typed essay, undated), p. 74.

more secure in his judgment: 'although she has agreed to the accusation, her own words might well be—should be—interpreted as words of self-condemnation' (p. 282). Bénichou seems to be even more convinced: 'Mais ces quelques vers, Phèdre ne les a pas voulus ambigus; dans son esprit, ils sont destinés à dénoncer sa propre faute, non à accuser Hippolyte'.[35]

Vera Orgel also feels that the Queen is denouncing herself, but is forced to admit that her speech 'bears the interpretation Œnone puts upon it'.[36] Venesoen goes still further, seeing in Phèdre's words an extension of the *mauvaise foi* he detects in the preceding scene: 'Ce silence, qui est aussi un art sournois de suggestion et de tromperie, se prolonge en présence de Thésée' (p. 174). Schérer's judgment is even more brutal: 'le silence de Phèdre est un crime' (p. 74); 'Phèdre participe activement, et non pas seulement par son silence, au plan d'Œnone, puisqu'elle dit à son mari: "Vous êtes offensée"' (p. 157). Pommier extends the criticism to include Phèdre's alleged hypocrisy ('l'art de préparer la voie à la calomnie, sans se calomnier soi-même'), seeing in her reply (which he describes as 'la réponse la plus calculée') further proof of the *mauvaise foi* which led her to claim in the previous scene that she was giving Œnone her head because she was incapable of acting for herself (pp. 218-19). Watching her on the stage, it will be obvious to all that Phèdre is acting under severe pressure as Thésée advances across the stage with the intention of embracing her. What is not at all clear from the script is whether the psychological pressure makes her flee with confused words of self-accusation, or whether it further undermines her moral integrity and actually persuades her to prepare the way for Œnone's calumny.

Racine indicates, in his preface, that she is suffering from 'une agitation d'esprit qui la met hors d'elle-même' and that she returns to the stage 'un moment après dans le dessein de justifier l'innocence et de déclarer la vérité'. As Maskell has pointed out, we know from the retrospective stage direction given in line 1196 ('Je volais toute entière au secours de son fils') that she comes rushing onto the stage: 'Speedy repentance is marked visually by her haste to speak to Thésée when she hears him quarrelling with Hippolyte' (p. 203). What is *not* clear, however, is how far she is prepared to go in order to save the maligned youth, since all she succeeds in doing is to appeal to Thésée's paternal feelings (1166-74). Abraham assumes that Phèdre is 'about to confess' (p. 122). Weinberg affirms similarly that 'Phèdre comes to Thésée in

---

[35] *L'Écrivain et ses travaux* (Paris, 1948), p. 318.

[36] *A New View of the Plays of Racine* (London, 1948), p. 185.

order to make a confession' (p. 261). The lines he quotes to prove this
are, however, far from conclusive:

> Je cédais au remords dont j'étais tourmentée.
> *Qui sait même où m'allait porter ce repentir?*
> *Peut-être* à m'accuser j'aurais pu consentir;
> *Peut-être*, si la voix ne m'eût été coupée,
> L'affreuse vérité *me serait échappée* (1200-1204; italics mine)

Phèdre's reticence here becomes even more significant if we bear in
mind the dramatic situation. The Queen is feeling angry at having been
spurned by Hippolyte and begins to adopt a tone more reminiscent of
Hermione: 'Ah, Dieux! Lorsqu'à mes vœux l'ingrat inexorable /
S'armait d'un œil si fier, d'un front si redoutable [...]'; 'Je suis le seul
objet qu'il ne saurait souffrir; / Et je me chargerais du soin de le
défendre?' (1205-1206, 1212-13). In this context, one would expect her
to exaggerate her commitment to saving him in order to make him
appear even more unworthy of her intervention on his behalf. Venesoen
is being too severe when he argues that Phèdre 'se [donne] l'illusion
d'avoir voulu secourir Hippolyte' (she did speak to Thésée) but he is
correct in affirming that 'elle ignore si elle aurait vraiment mis fin [à
son] malheur' (p. 176). More significantly, we in the audience are left in
similar ignorance.

When Philip Butler suggests that Phèdre's behaviour would be
unforgivable if it were not for the fact that she immediately went to see
Thésée in order to save his son,[37] he is obviously referring to the scene
just discussed. In terms of attempting to determine Phèdre's guilt,
however, one might legitimately ask what efforts she makes to save
Hippolyte in the subsequent scenes. Butler, almost certainly, does not do
so because he feels that, once Hippolyte has been cursed, all attempts to
save him are doomed to failure (p. 75). This would seem to be
supported by Thésée's assertion:

> Misérable, tu cours à ta perte infaillible.
> Un dieu vengeur te suit, tu ne peux l'éviter. (1157-8)

One notes, however, that, once he begins to suspect that Hippolyte is
innocent, Thésée prays to Neptune begging him not to 'précipite[r] [ses]
funestes bienfaits' (1483). This may or may not be realistic: my point,
once again, is that the script leaves the issue unclear.[38] One could argue,

---

[37] *A Student's Guide to Racine* (London, 1974), p. 82.

[38] The ambiguity is essential if Racine is to achieve suspense between the end of Act IV and the end of Act V.

in any case, that the more vital issue is not whether objectively there is any chance of saving Hippolyte but how Phèdre herself responds to the news that Neptune has been asked to take his life. She is certainly shocked ('Neptune vous la doit! Quoi? vos vœux irrités [...]', (1179)); but she is cut off in mid-speech by her angry husband. Thereafter, she refers both to the possibility of exile (1255) and to the possibility of death. She seems to think, indeed, that Hippolyte may *already* be dead. Thus, rebuking Œnone, she cries:

> Pourquoi ta bouche impie
> A-t-elle, en l'accusant, osé noircir sa vie?
> Il en mourra peut-être, et d'un père insensé
> Le sacrilège vœu peut-être est exaucé. (1313-6)

Once again, it is difficult to know how to interpret the script here. Phèdre may genuinely believe that Hippolyte is dead but, given the particular dramatic context (wishing to vilify Œnone, she will naturally adopt the most extreme interpretation of the situation), she may well be exaggerating.

The ambiguity extends into the next act when she takes a (relatively) slow-acting poison before returning to the stage in scene vii. Hippolyte's death has been announced to Thésée by Théramène in scene vi. Hippolyte's mentor will certainly not have ventured into the palace in order to see the Queen before seeing the young man's father. This, no doubt, is why Abraham does not hesitate to affirm that Phèdre takes the poison before learning of Hippolyte's death (p. 133). We have no way of knowing for certain, however, that someone else has not transmitted the news.[39] Dédéyan argues that the issue is not really important: 'Qu'importe [?] la mort suspendue sur son amant provoque son dernier geste, sa confession et sa réparation finale' (p. 63). Pommier, however, feels that it is crucial: 'Qu'on y prenne garde! de la réponse à cette question dépend le jugement qu'il faut prononcer sur cette femme' (p. 220). It would obviously be simplistic to suggest that our view of Phèdre should be solely (or even predominantly) determined by her actions in the last act. But her behaviour there is important since, had Hippolyte still been alive, it would have been her last chance to put matters right. Pommier feels that, if Phèdre knows that the object of her passion is dead, then she is probably acting like Hermione, 'qui persiste dans sa fureur en refusant de survivre'. Alternatively, if she feels that

---

[39] It has often been pointed out that the time allowed between Hippolyte's exit at line 1410 and Théramène's announcement of his death at line 1491 ff. is hardly realistic. In these circumstances, speculation about whether Phèdre has or has not been told is unlikely to be fruitful.

there might still be time to save him, then she might well be acting, *in extremis*, in an eminently altruistic way, sacrificing her own life and reputation in order to permit Hippolyte to be happy with Aricie: 'en déclarant l'innocence de sa victime, elle finit l'exil et permit la réunion' (p. 200). Had Racine given Phèdre the opportunity to speak when she enters at line 1594, he would have given us the opportunity to answer Dédéyan's question. By having Thésée blurt out the news of Hippolyte's death, he deliberately cultivates ambiguity.

Usually with Racine, one knows that careful scrutiny of the text / script will reveal information which explains his plot. In *Phèdre* the protagonist's identification of Hippolyte with his father in Act II, scene v is prepared by her reference to his resemblance to Thésée in Act I, scene iii (289-90). Likewise, in *Iphigénie*, the question of Ériphile's true identity is hinted at early in the play (427-30). Gordon Pocock does not hesitate to argue, therefore, that: 'When so much seems to hang on a point on which Racine gives us no certain information, it is clear we are seeking to understand his effects in the wrong way' (p. 238). I hope that it is apparent from the above that this judgement is *not* applicable to *Phèdre*: Racine, who has such frequent recourse to ambiguity, is deliberately attempting to increase the ambiguity of his heroine. In many ways, the question 'How guilty is Phèdre?' (which is obviously central to the play) is meaningless because the script contains too many uncertainties and variables for us even to start to offer a convincing answer.

There are three crucial occasions, however, when regarding the play as theatre helps us to arrive at a more precise assessment of Phèdre's guilt or innocence. To take innocence first, Schérer argues that Phèdre's failure to inform Thésée in Act IV of what has really passed between her and Hippolyte is part of her 'crime' (pp. 74-5). Venesoen makes the same point, relating her weakness to her jealousy (p. 176), as does Weinberg, who argues that, thought we do not blame Phèdre for falling in love, we do blame her 'for allowing that love to turn to jealousy and for permitting jealousy to overcome justice' (p. 296). They would seem to be supported in this judgment by Harry Barnwell: 'It is Phèdre's possessive passion for Hippolyte that drives her to her jealous refusal to exculpate him in the eyes of Thésée'.[40] Picard writes that, 'ivre de jalousie, Phèdre s'en va sans avoir rien dit' (p. 740). Any director would immediately point out to Picard that Phèdre does not leave the stage in Act IV scene iv: *Thésée* exits, leaving Phèdre alone with her

---

[40] *The Tragic Drama of Corneille and Racine* (Oxford, 1982), p. 242.

jealousy, which soon turns to self-recrimination and then anger against Œnone. Pommier tells us that Phèdre is so thunderstruck by Thésée's revelation concerning Aricie that she no longer listens to him: 'La terrible nouvelle abat Phèdre à ce point que Thésée n'a plus d'interlocutrice' (p. 197). This is a very sensitive reading of the text, but the director would also try to show on stage that her husband is so caught up in his own emotions that *he is not attempting to relate to Phèdre*. He interrupts her at line 1180, and, having astounded her with the allegedly false story concerning Aricie at line 1188, gives her only the briefest of opportunities to react before rushing off at line 1192. Judging Phèdre in her dramatic context here, it is evident that she is rooted to the spot, paralysed by Thésée's unexpected revelation, whilst he is moved by his self-generating anger. If blame is to be bestowed on a character in Act IV, scene iv, it could quite fittingly be bestowed on Thésée, who acts so impulsively.

There is not scope for an analysis here of the role of Thésée; but it should be obvious that Phèdre will not be judged in isolation. Insofar as Thésée comes across as a mundane, morally inadequate figure,[41] Phèdre with her crimes but also with her highly developed moral consciousness will appear all the more impressive. Insofar as he is portrayed as a mythical hero, guilty of *hamartia* but not deserving of the fate which he, Neptune and Phèdre prepare for him, he may well appear to be a 'strikingly impressive tragic figure'.[42] Once again, one cannot stress too much the importance of the role of the director.

The role of the director will equally be crucial where Œnone is concerned. She has, ever since Racine's preface, tended to receive a bad press. Pommier, for instance, sees her as a 'Narcisse femelle' and emphasises her own intense dislike of Hippolyte (pp. 216-17). But she could easily be directed, as Maulnier has pointed out, in a much more sympathetic way: 'Je la vois caressant Phèdre, la pressant dans ses bras, berçant sa douleur, vivant à travers Phèdre l'amour de Phèdre dans une complicité presque sensuelle [...] qui est celle de l'identification maternelle' (p. 159). Once again, Racine's script is too ambiguous to allow us to say which of these two views is the more 'accurate'. What the script does do, however, is force us to question the accuracy of Phèdre's criticisms of her nurse in Act IV, scene vi and Act V, scene vii.

Whether Œnone is directed as she would be by Short, as a 'mean-spirited human being' (p. 71), or as the 'double maternel de Phèdre', as

---

[41] Abraham sees him as a 'self-righteous fool' (p. 126).

[42] Pocock, p. 239.

she would be by Barthes (p. 116), the audience is for once fully aware
of at least one thing: whatever the ambiguity surrounding her intentions
(see above pp. 119-20), when Phèdre pronounced the fatal words 'Fais
ce que tu voudras', she gave Œnone to understand that she could proceed
with her plan to accuse Hippolyte. There is in this sense no escaping
from Phèdre's objective guilt. To what extent does she accept it? To
what extent does she use her criticisms of Œnone in order to reduce her
own feelings of guilt?

Weinberg quotes the relevant lines from Acts IV and V (1307-14,
1625-30) and comments that they are 'not only summations of the kind
Racine had frequently used to render his action perspicuous to his
audience' but also represent Phèdre's 'estimate of the respective
responsibilities' (p. 286). Once again, however, it is vital to remember
that we are dealing here with a character who finds herself in a
particular dramatic context. In Act IV, she has just recovered from the
paroxysm of jealousy which led her to wish that Aricie should be killed,
but has immediately plunged into a fit of remorse which has again left
her suicidal. In this context, Œnone's comment to the effect that love is a
normal human weakness and that she should 'regarde[r] d'un autre œil
une excusable erreur' (1296) is certainly poorly timed but not in itself
unreasonable.[43] It is clearly motivated, in any case, by Œnone's constant
desire to save her mistress's life (773-4). The audience should be
shocked, therefore, at the violence of Phèdre's response:

> Qu'entends-je? Quels conseils ose-t-on me donner?
> Ainsi donc jusqu'au bout tu veux m'empoisonner,
> Malheureuse? [...]

This tirade might have been justified in Act III when Œnone suggested
falsely accusing Hippolyte, but seems excessive here. The audience, in
consequence, should be alert to the need to assess the accuracy of
Phèdre's criticisms (which are far from being objective 'summations' of
the plot). 'Au jour que je fuyais c'est toi qui m'a rendue' is obviously
justified; but 'Tes prières m'ont fait oublier mon devoir' is more
ambiguous. 'Devoir' is used by the Queen here to refer to the obligation
to die expressed in Act I (217); but she glibly passes over Œnone's
redefinition of her duty ('Mais ce nouveau malheur vous prescrit
d'autres lois', (340)) when she argued that, following Thésée's alleged
death, Phèdre had a duty to protect her sons (355-62): a redefinition of

---

[43] Odette de Mourgues describes Œnone's statement as 'most amoral' (*Racine or the Triumph of Relevance* (Cambridge, 1967), p. 108). Pocock, on the other hand, suggests that it should perhaps be regarded as 'humane and sympathetic' (p. 254).

her duty which, at the time, the Queen had apparently accepted (363-6). The accusation 'J'évitais Hippolyte, et tu me l'as fait voir' is, consequently, a gross oversimplification. As for her despairing questions ('De quoi te chargeais-tu? Pourquoi ta bouche impie / A-t-elle, en l'accusant, osé noircir sa vie?'), one is inevitably reminded of Hermoine's famous: 'Qui te l'a dit?'. Even as Phèdre attempts to accentuate Œnone's responsibility by insisting on the possibly fatal consequences of her intervention ('Il en mourra peut-être'), the audience is inevitably reminded of the nurse's striking (because unexpected) admission that her plan might result in Hippolyte's death ('Mais le sang innocent dût-il être versé [...]' —903). Phèdre is evidently transferring her own unbearable sense of guilt to her nurse. The latter is not innocent, but she is not as guilty as Phèdre here pretends. This should be quite clear to the reader of the text, but will be even clearer to an audience, which will be much more forcibly exposed to the sheer ferocity of Phèdre's dismissal of Œnone, and much more directly affected by the latter's distressed tone as she exits: 'Ah! Dieux! pour la servir j'ai tout fait, tout quitté; / Et j'en reçois ce prix? Je l'ai bien mérité' (1327-8).

The question of how far the repentant Phèdre is prepared to go in accepting and confessing her guilt will, therefore, be uppermost in the spectators' minds as Act V begins. We have already noted that the Queen tells her nurse that Hippolyte is *perhaps* already dead. Given the ambiguity already discussed above (pp. 118-19) concerning the reversibility of Thésée's curse, we might reasonably expect Phèdre to try to intervene once more. Butler, however, writes: 'she will, in a trance of jealousy, almost absent-mindedly, let Hippolyte die' (p. 76). What she is suffering from at this point is not jealousy but the guilt caused by her desire to have Aricie killed, which she cannot so easily shuffle off onto Œnone. This said, the description of Phèdre as almost absent-mindedly allowing fate to take its course seems most appropriate. Her guilt so preoccupies her that, apart from her children (1471-4), she can think of nothing else. She obviously needs to confess, but, as we can deduce from Panope's *récit*, cannot find the words to express herself by letter (1477-8). In the event, she takes poison and, with death now being just a matter of time, should now be able to provide a true account of events. But does she? She certainly admits that it was she who fell in love with Hippolyte and not he with her (1617-19, 1623-4). Her criticisms of the malevolence of the gods so evident in the earlier part of the play (e.g. 249-50, 257-8) now give way to a single line ('Le ciel mit dans mon sein une flamme funeste'), which seems to imply that whatever happened thereafter was very much a question of human responsibility. The guilt, however, is once again transferred to Œnone: 'La détestable Œnone a conduit tout le reste'. The audience, however, knows that the nurse, who was addressed as 'chère Œnone' earlier in the play (153), had every reason to believe that she had been given permission to accuse Hippolyte.[44] The account offered by Phèdre ('La perfide, abusant de ma faiblesse extrême, / S'est hâtée à vos yeux de l'accuser lui-même') accurately reflects Phèdre's physical weakness and panic earlier in the play; but it does not do justice to what the audience has seen happen on the stage at the most crucial point in the drama.

We may now recognise a pattern that has been slowly emerging. When first confessing her passion to Œnone, Phèdre uses a periphrasis to refer to Hippolyte ('ce fils de l'Amazone'), but, when Œnone correctly identifies him, she blames her for mentioning his name: 'C'est toi qui l'as nommé' (262-4). In Act III, scene i, when Œnone is urging her to suppress her passion, the Queen accuses her of encouraging her passion: 'Par tes conseils flatteurs tu m'as su ranimer. / Tu m'as fait entrevoir que je pouvais l'aimer' (771-2). The reference is to line 350, when Œnone believing Thésée to be dead, argues 'Votre flamme devient une flamme ordinaire'. What Phèdre omits to say was that this was but a part of a much more complex argument. (Now that Thésée is dead, you can see Hippolyte with less risk to yourself—and you need to since, as a result of your antagonistic behaviour, you may have alienated Hippolyte to the point where he will act against your sons, who, in the new political situation are extremely vulnerable (340 ff.)). In Act III, scene iii, Phèdre is equally unfair. Now that Thésée is known to be alive, her situation is evidently worse but it does not justify the accusation:

> Sur mes justes remords tes pleurs ont prévalu.
> Je mourais ce matin digne d'être pleurée;
> J'ai suivi tes conseils, je meurs déshonorée. (836-8)

Whilst it is true that, had Phèdre died before seeing Hippolyte, she would not have dishonoured herself, the only reason why Phèdre is now dishonoured is because she confessed her love to him. As the audience must be abundantly aware, Œnone never advised this: it was Phèdre's own lack of self-control which betrayed her. Her increasingly paranoid reactions reach a climax in Act IV not only in the tirade already analysed but also earlier in the same scene when, imagining that Hippolyte and Aricie have been having frequent meetings, she accuses Œnone not only of knowing this and not telling her ('Tu le savais') but

---

[44] Note, in particular, her injunction 'Mais ne me trompez point, vous est-il cher encore?' and, of course her warning that the consequences of her plan might be fatal (882, 903-8).

also, even more irrationally, of somehow allowing her to fall in love with her stepson: 'Pourquoi me laissais-tu séduire?' (1231-3). Alerted by the recurring distortions of events and conversations which the audience has witnessed, the spectators are finally in a position to judge at least one aspect of Phèdre's guilt. We cannot know exactly what she meant when she said 'Fais ce que tu voudras' in Act III. We cannot know how far she intended to go when pleading with Thésée to spare Hippolyte in Act IV. Likewise, we cannot know whether she knew that Hippolyte was already dead when she came to see Thésée in Act V. We do know, however, that, despite the loathing with which she regards her passion, she has allowed herself to become embroiled in a series of events which have caused the young man's death. Her own feelings of guilt seem to reach their paroxysm in Act IV when, having merely thought of having Aricie killed, she has recoiled in horror at her own crimes and resolved once more to die (1264-77). Unable to face Minos without having previously confessed her guilt to Thésée, she finds that she cannot do so unless she is certain of the imminence of her death: hence the poison.[45] Even then, she cannot quite bring herself to tell the whole truth. In Goldmann's terms,[46] she has the opportunity to consolidate her tragic stature as she confesses and turns her back on an impure world. Perhaps her ultimate tragedy is that, as the play reaches its dramatic climax, Phèdre just fails to free herself of the impurities from which she would, indeed, have dearly loved to escape. Even in death, she is 'ni tout à fait coupable, ni tout à fait innocente'.

---

[45] Abraham is quite wrong to affirm that she did not have to take poison before confessing (p. 133). In Bidar, Phèdre takes her life only *after* she has confessed (Pommier, p. 202).

[46] *Le Dieu caché* (Paris, 1959), p. 423.

Seventeenth-century French Studies: an appraisal

It is a truth universally acknowledged that a *dix-septièmiste* in possession of good teaching skills must be in want of redeployment. Over per cent of Universities and nearly all the Polytechnics and Colleges of Technology which have just acquired University status give no place to seventeenth-century French studies. Out of 111 posts advertised recently, only one specified an interest in seventeenth-century literature. The crisis of identity affecting the Humanities, and in particular the study of French, is causing a re-examination of the subject (witness the first transbinary conference, *French in the 1990s*, held at the University of Birmingham in July 1991). The aim of this paper is to set in motion a *table ronde* on the present state of seventeenth-century French studies in British Universities and on the particular challenges facing our discipline.

Responses to questionnaires sent to 53 established British Universities (the New Universities were excluded as these had not at the time received official recognition) have given an indication of changes which have taken place over the last twenty years. The survey is based on returns from 50 Universities.[1]

1. How many *dix-septièmistes* were there in your University / College?

in 1991-92?	70
10 years ago?	93
20 years ago?	95[2]

---

[1] I am very grateful to colleagues completing the questionnaire; some undertook quasi-archival research to provide answers.

[2] Records are incomplete but the figure has been arrived at from lists of personnel for 1971-72.

Universities without *dix-septièmistes* in:

1991-92	15
10 years ago	8
20 years ago	10

These figures indicate those with a teaching and / or research interest in seventeenth-century studies. However, a number of 'pure *dix-septièmistes*' have been heavily committed in administration; others have had to spread themselves over other fields. In Oxford and Cambridge, the reverse tendency is seen, with colleagues whose primary research interests lie elsewhere lecturing and writing on topics relating to the seventeenth century. Nevertheless the loss of around twenty-five per cent of *dix-septièmistes* over the last ten years is proportionate to losses sustained by other specialisms. The age profile (with the vast majority of *dix-septièmistes* in the 45-55 range), while not inconsistent with the national average for French Departments, has serious implications for the future of the discipline.

The ominous signs are reflected in the disappearance of seventeenth-century studies from the syllabi of seven Universities over the last ten years. Some *dix-septièmistes* expressed fears with regard to the demise of their subject with their retirement.

2. In your University / College are seventeenth-century French studies?

Compulsory?	2
Optional?	38
Not taught at all?	10

If optional, How would you describe the take-up?

Low?	4
Average?	23
High?	11

Nine Universities have a compulsory seventeenth-century course for first- or second-year students. In one University seventeenth-century French studies are compulsory for Single Honours but optional for Joint Honours. Next year one of the largest Universities will be reverting to a compulsory seventeenth-century element as part of a paper called 'Introduction to French literary texts from 1450 to the present day'.

The difficulty in evaluating this section of the questionnaire lies in determining the points of comparison. 'Average' sometimes meant 'average for a pre-seventeenth-century course'; 'low' was on one occasion in comparison with twentieth-century literature; 'high' was sometimes due to the personal qualities of the *dix-septièmiste* rather than to the intrinsic appeal of the subject.

3. Which texts / authors / anthologies were studied:

In 1991-92?

35	Molière
35	Racine
32	Corneille
25	*La Princesse de Clèves*
18	Pascal
15	La Fontaine
11	Descartes
8	La Rochefoucauld
5	La Bruyère
4	Madame de Sévigné
3	Saint Simon
2	Guilleragues (*Les Portugaises*)
2	Perrault (*Les Contes*)
2	Poetry
2	Regnard
2	Rotrou
2	Boileau
1	Bayle
1	Bossuet
1	Cyrano
1	Quinault
1	Saint-Évremond
1	Sorel
1	Tristan
1	Blunt: Art and Architecture in France 1500-1950
1	Church and Society in France 1630-1700
1	Culture and Society in Seventeenth-Century France (Fénelon, Saint-Simon, Madame de Sévigné)
1	The Cultural Heritage of Modern France (Sixteenth-Eighteenth Centuries)
1	Literature, Thought and Society in the Seventeenth Century

10 years ago? (if known)

34	Molière
33	Racine
31	Corneille
23	*La Princesse de Clèves*
19	Pascal
19	La Fontaine
12	Descartes
12	La Rochefoucauld
8	La Bruyère
3	Théophile
3	Boileau
2	Bossuet
2	Cyrano
2	Fénelon
2	Mme de Sévigné
2	*Moralistes*
2	Poetry
2	Rotrou
1	Corneille (Thomas)
1	Fontenelle
1	Méré
1	Quinault
1	Sorel
1	Church and Society in France 1630-1700
1	Classical Period
1	Seventeenth-Century Rhetoricians
1	Satirists (Anthology)

20 years ago? (if known)[3]

27	Molière
26	Racine
26	Corneille
21	Pascal
18	*La Princesse de Clèves*
14	La Fontaine
13	Descartes
10	La Rochefoucauld

---

[3] Records are incomplete.

3	La Bruyère
3	*Libertins*
3	Poetry
2	*Moralistes*
2	Tristan
2	Regnard
1	Desmarets de Saint-Sorlin
1	Mairet
1	Rotrou
1	Scarron
1	Extracts from *L'Astrée, Le Roman comique, Le Roman bourgeois*
1	Superstition in Seventeenth-Century France
1	Survey of Seventeenth-Century Literature

The predominance of the dramatists reveals the narrowness of the canon. The growth of interest in *La Princesse de Clèves* and in Madame de Sévigné could be attributed to the feminist influence. The profile in France is markedly different. As Christophe Campos has shown in his recent analysis of exam questions (*French in the 90s* (Birmingham, 1992), p. 131) 'baroque poets and mid-century radicals and reformers are in the ascendant'. The dramatists too are regarded differently in French Universities: 'Corneille is practically only known for his comedies and very late complex tragedies, Racine is under a cloud, and Molière is studied more for his farce than his philosophy'. In British Universities attention is given to Corneille's early tetralogy and *Le Menteur*; Molière's 'philosphical' or 'problem' texts (e.g. *L'École des femmes, Tartuffe, Dom Juan* and *Le Misanthrope*); and 'traditionally "major" and "minor" members of the Racine canon' (Campos, ibid.).

4. Which texts / authors have been best received by students?

32	Molière
28	Racine
16	Corneille
12	*La Princesse de Clèves*
5	La Fontaine
4	Pascal
2	Descartes
1	Cyrano
1	Fénelon
1	Mme de Sévigné

1   Saint-Simon
1   Seventeenth-Century Art
     The Anthology of Satirists (including La Fontaine, La Bruyère and Boileau) did well in one University (but has disappeared from the syllabus!).

Various reasons may be advanced for the winners and losers: personal factors, accessibility, the relatively low cost of certain texts. The *moralistes* and philosophical works had a small but enthusiastic following but were generally found to be heavy going.

5. Has the approach to the teaching of seventeenth-century French studies changed in your University / College?

No (or little) change:
5 reported no change over the last 20 years.
1 indicated 'no change', except for the recent addition of Barthes and Goldmann to the Racine Bibliography.
Some reported cosmetic changes or a change of nomenclature (e.g. 'Seventeenth-Century Literature' renamed 'Literature under Louis XIV').

Significant changes:
Five factors have led to the restructuring of courses and to the disappearance of certain authors / texts (particularly philosophical works):

i) Optionality:
Many courses are taught in Special Subjects. This has generally led to concentration on specific texts / authors rather than on major historical / literary surveys of the century. Many texts are no longer taught as part of a historical sequence studied by all students. The time allocated has invariably been reduced. Accessibility has been considered crucial in choosing texts.

ii) Loss of specialists:
A further restriction has been imposed by the particular aptitudes and interests of the 'retrained' *dix-septièmistes*.

iii) Unavailability of texts:
This has further limited the scope for introducing secondary authors. In the discussion which followed it was suggested that members of the

Society could pool resources to make generally available hand-outs of texts (particularly of the *moralistes* and philosophers) which had been well received.

iv) The abandoning of periodisation:

    a) In favour of reading strategies;

    b) In favour of a 'topic based' or thematic approach (e.g. 'The rise of the Individual in ...'; 'Myth').

v) Method:

    a) The introduction of new approaches (particularly by new appointees).

    b) The move away from lectures to seminars.

    c) The use of video (particularly in the teaching of drama).

    d) Greater emphasis on *mise-en-scène* (with encouragement given to students to see live performances).

6. What of the future? The mood amongst *dix-septièmistes* revealed sharply divergent reactions. Many expressed a sense of foreboding, in view of the organisational changes within their Universities and the general flight from literature:

> If we have other strings to our bow we shall be asked to use them.

> As background knowledge of the students (historical, religious, literary) becomes more limited the appeal of seventeenth-century literature becomes harder to convey to students.

> I view the future of seventeenth-century French studies at my own University with profound pessimism.

> Seventeenth-century studies are somewhat marginalised, in terms of numbers, by increasing emphasis on matters modern, political and institutional.

> The demise of seventeenth-century studies in 5-10 years is only to be envisaged in the context of a move away from all literature in French.

> Modularisation will hasten the decline.

Another reaction was of uncertainty:

> The future is rather uncertain under our present Head of Department but I hope we shall be able to 'fly the flag' for a while longer.

One colleague seemed possessed of the ataraxia of La Mothe le Vayer, or perhaps was contemplating early retirement:

> Students find seventeenth-century literature less accessible nowadays. But this does not perturb me.

Student detachment was emphasised in another return:

> I now feel that students feel much more remote from the Seventeenth Century than twenty years ago, but aren't obviously bothered by it.

Two colleagues were content to enjoy a stay of execution:

> I can see no danger that the present provision will diminish so long as the present *dix-septièmiste* is in post. After that—curtains.

> Medieval, Sixteenth Century and Eighteenth Century have vanished from the syllabus. While I don't think that when I go a seventeenth-century specialist will be appointed here, until such an evil day, the Seventeenth Century is faring 'well': it survives, alone of its kind.

There were however grounds for (albeit guarded) optimism:

> The Seventeenth Century goes fairly well.

> The future looks a little brighter after revamping.

> Seventeenth-century studies are surviving, and are proving popular with students.

In some Universities the mood was positively buoyant:

> The second most popular course in the Department.

> Certainly, one of the most popular courses (with students).

> One of the most over-subscribed courses; in fact, a rate-capping exercise had to be introduced to divert students to other 'less popular' subjects.

> There is life in the *Grand Siècle* yet.

A common concern was the lack of research students, particularly in some of the traditional centres of research which are still managing to attract postgraduates in other literary disciplines (including Medieval and Renaissance). Many reasons may be cited: the image the period projects, the widespread but erroneous notion that there is no research left to be done, the shift in focus away from traditional scholarship to the sometimes disorientating and arcane '-isms' which critics love to belabour. Above all, we need to reckon with the job opportunities factor—we have to counsel potential supervisees of the need to consider the modern specialisms preferred in job advertisements. However, far from being exclusive to the U.K. the problem is encountered in French Universities. It would be interesting to find out whether a similar situation exists in the U.S.A.

Whither Seventeenth-century French studies? In one sense, the crisis is *sub specie modernitatis*. Our discipline has fared as well as or even better than other pre-twentieth-century studies. However, in the current market-driven educational environment the task of persuading a 'clientele', schooled in the utilitarian and the user-friendly, of the value of studying works of art whose well-defined parameters defy instant access will remain a difficult one. Two extreme positions may be adopted: the glib, pseudo-rhetoric of the ad-man or the showman, ironically the very *persona* which the period's culture holds up to ridicule or to abuse; or the proud, post-rationalised inertia of La Fontaine's fox, prompted by his inability to reach the grapes to which he aspires:

> Mais comme il n'y pouvait atteindre:
> 'Ils sont trop verts, dit-il, et bons pour des goujats'.
> Fit-il pas mieux que de se plaindre?
> *(Le Renard et les raisins* (III, ii))

All the evidence points to there being no one solution. It has proved both administratively impossible and politically undesirable to keep subjects at a fixed parity in some kind of curricular exchange-rate mechanism. But does this suggest that a free-for-all, in which students are refusing what they do not know, is necessarily the best alternative? The political climate, and indeed intellectual fashions, may change. However, for the immediate future, fundamental questions remain: can we envisage a degree in French without Molière and Racine or a degree in English Literature without Shakespeare? Can we teach seventeenth-century French studies without any reference to the distinctive intellectual achievements of the *Grand Siècle*? Many would say yes. It will be for future generations of students to decide, and for us as teachers to endeavour to ensure that their choice is as informed as we can make it.[4]

---

[4] The lively debate which followed was, regrettably, not recorded. It was hoped that this item would remain on the agenda of the Society for Seventeenth-Century French Studies, and would be further explored at a future conference.

Contributors

CHRISTOPHER SMITH is Reader in French at the University of East Anglia and was the founding editor of *Seventeenth-Century French Studies*.

CLAIRE PACE is Lecturer in History of Art at the University of Glasgow. Her numerous publications include a book on Nicholas Poussin.

ELIZABETH MOLES is Lecturer in French at the University of Glasgow, and has written a number of scholarly articles on Pascal, Montaigne, and Saint-Amant.

WILLIAM DICKSON is Senior Lecturer in French at the University of Glasgow and is currently engaged on a study of the rhetoric of Pierre Corneille. His publications include an edition of Scarron's *Le Jodelet ou le maistre valet* (1986).

ROBERT McBRIDE is Professor of French at the New University of Ulster, Coleraine. His many publications include *Aspects of Seventeenth-century French Drama and Thought* (1979), *The Sceptical Vision of Molière: a study in paradox* (1977) and *The Triumph of Ballet in Molière's Theatre* (1992).

NICHOLAS CRONK is Fellow and Dean of St Edmund Hall, Oxford. He has published widely on seventeenth- and eighteenth-century literature, and has two articles forthcoming on Molière-Charpentier's *Le Malade imaginaire*

CHRISTINE McGARRY is research student and tutorial assistant at the University of Glasgow, and is currently completing a thesis entitled 'Aspects of Time in Racinian Tragedy'.

RICHARD PARISH is Fellow and Senior Tutor of St Catherine's College, Oxford. His numerous publications include *Pascal's 'Lettres provinciales': a study in polemic* (1989); a major study on Racine is shortly to appear.

JAMES J. SUPPLE is Senior Lecturer at the University of St Andrews. His publications include *Arms versus letters: the military and literary ideals in the 'Essais' of Montaigne* (1984), and *Racine: 'Bérénice'* (1986).

NOËL PEACOCK is Senior Lecturer in French and Head of Department at the University of Glasgow. Publications include editions of Molière, *La Jalousie du Barbouillé & George Dandin* (1984) and *Dépit amoureux* (1989), and critical guides, *Molière: 'L'École des femmes'* (1988) and *Molière: 'Les Femmes savantes'* (1990). Forthcoming is *Molière in Scotland, 1945-1990*.

UNIVERSITY OF GLASGOW
FRENCH AND GERMAN PUBLICATIONS

French Department, The University.   Glasgow G12 8QL, Scotland, G.B.

Collections of Essays

Words of Power:
Essays in Honour of Alison Fairlie
edited by Dorothy G. Coleman and Gillian Jondorf
£12.00
ISBN 0 85261 209 5

Henri Marel
'Germinal': une documentation intégrale
textes réunis et édités par Geoff Woollen
£11.00
SBN 0 85261 248 6

Zola: 'La Bête humaine': texte et explications
actes du colloque du centenaire, 1990, édités par Geoff Woollen
£11.00
ISBN 0 85261 279 6

Voices in the Air:
French dramatists and the resources of language
essays presented to Professor Charles Chadwick
£15.00
ISBN 0 85261 340 7

Emblems in Glasgow
a collection of essays drawing on the Stirling Maxwell Collection
edited by Alison Adams
£9.50
ISBN 0 85261 347 4

France Free and Unfree: the literary and sociological image
edited by William Craw (in preparation)
£7.50
ISBN 0 85261 369 5

Post paid. Cheques payable to 'University of Glasgow', account 114502.

Glasgow Introductory Guides to French Literature

1.	Camus : La Peste	Edward J. Hughes
2.	Molière : L'École des femmes	Noël Peacock
3.	Balzac : Le Curé de Tours	Geoff Woollen
4.	Sartre : Les Mains sales	Paul Reed
5.	Cesbron : Chiens perdus sans collier Cardinal : La Clé sur la porte	Colin Roberts
6.	Maupassant : Boule de Suif	Peggy Chaplin
7.	Anouilh : Becket	Edmund Smyth
8.	Colette : Le Blé en herbe	Jean Duffy
9.	Pagnol : L'Eau des collines	David Coward
10.	Ernaux : La Place / Une femme	Loraine Day & Tony Jones
11.	Zola : Thérèse Raquin	Claude Schumacher
12.	Beauvoir : Les Belles Images / La Femme rompue	Terry Keefe
13.	Zola : L'Assommoir	Roger Clark
14.	Tournier : La Goutte d'or	Michael Worton
15.	Tournier : Vendredi	Margaret-Anne Hutton
16.	Racine : Andromaque	Peter France
17.	Molière : Le Misanthrope	David Whitton
18.	Vercors : Le Silence de la mer	William Kidd
19.	Laclos: Les Liaisons dangereuses	Philip Thody
20.	Structuralism : Theory and Practice	Jean Duffy
21.	Camus : L'Étranger	G.V. Banks
22.	Proust : Du côté de chez Swann	Michael Wetherill
23.	Verne : Le Tour du monde en 80 jours	Timothy Unwin